# *Post-War* KITCHEN

Nostalgic Food and Facts from 1945–1954

BY **Marguerite Patten** O.B.E.

# *Post-War* KITCHEN

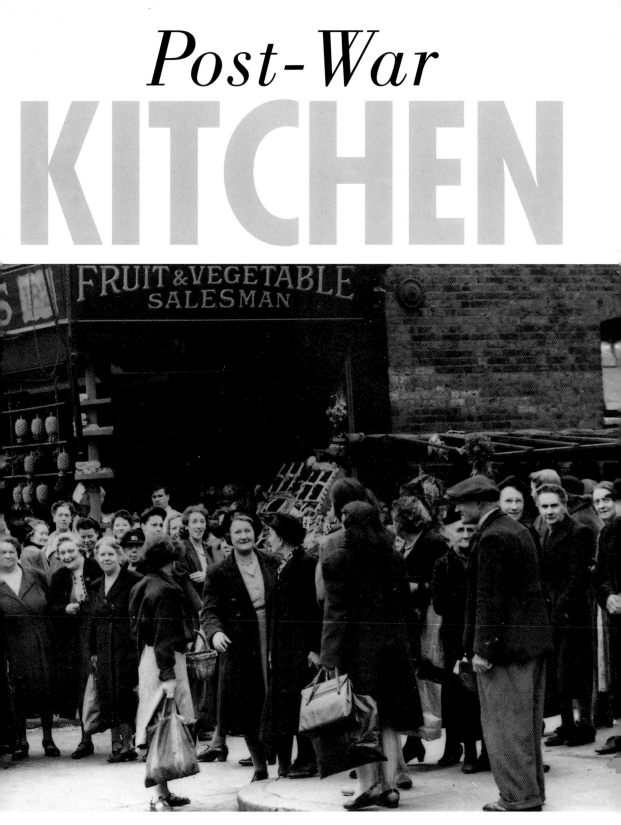

hamlyn

First published in 1998
by Hamlyn
a division of Octopus Publishing Group Limited
2-4 Heron Quays, London,  E14 4JP

Reprinted in 1998, 2000, 2001 and 2002

ISBN 0 600 60255 9

Note: Both imperial and metric measurements have been given in all recipes.
Use one set of measurements only and not a mixture of both.

# CONTENTS

# ★ THE END OF THE WAR ★

I am sure everyone can appreciate the feelings of relief and exhilaration felt in 1945 throughout Britain as well as in the Empire (as the Commonwealth was still called) and in the countries of our other Allies. The war had been won, we were justifiably proud of our victories and enjoyed celebrating them. After the celebrations, though, it became time to 'pick up the pieces' and return to a normal life again, as it had been in 1939 before the war began.

The next years were to show that it was not as easy as might have been imagined to return to the *status quo* of 1939. First, there was a desperate shortage of food throughout the world. In countries that had been conquered by Germany and Japan people were starving. This meant that in Britain we had to accept continued food rationing. In 1945, we had no idea that it would be 1954 before the last of the controlled foods became derationed.

This book deals with the kind of dishes we prepared from 1945 to 1954. As each group of foods came off ration it meant fascinating changes in the recipes we were using. In spite of rationing, though, our way of regarding meals was different from what it had been in wartime. We were more carefree and we entertained more. A greater variety of unrationed foods gradually became available; we welcomed imported fruits and vegetables to augment home-grown varieties.

**W**HILE WE WERE still thinking longingly in the years from 1945 of good pre-war succulent roast joints and tender steaks, there were slight changes in attitude about the kind of food we wanted. People from many nations had been in Britain, either serving in the forces or here as refugees; they had met British people and told them about their national dishes. Then, too, British men and women had served in the armed forces in many countries and they had gleaned some knowledge of various foreign cuisines. Gradually, as we moved into the 1950s, more people started to holiday abroad. All of these factors made us more willing to accept new kinds of food and different types of cooking side by side with our own traditional fare.

Most people had been grateful to the Ministry of Food for its work during the war years. The Ministry had given practical information and recipes in newspapers, on the radio and in demonstrations throughout the country. It had helped people make the best of the restricted foods available. The people at the Ministry felt, quite rightly, that they had kept the population at home healthy during the war years. They now decided that they should continue to guide and advise us on what we should, or should not, eat in the years ahead. The Ministry's experts published *The A.B.C. of Cooking* for general sale and monthly booklets entitled *Food and Nutrition* for use by educational establishments.

After a year or so of such work many people became disenchanted with the Ministry's continual advice and there were mutterings about Britain being turned into a 'nanny-state'. People wanted restrictions lifted and rationing to end as speedily as possible so that they would to be able to buy just what they wanted and not what they were told was good for them.

It was not just the attitude to food that had changed with the war. Although many men and women from the forces were happy to return to their peacetime occupations, others were less willing to do so. In spite of the dangers of war, they had seen new countries and had experienced a more exciting life which they wanted to find at home. Perhaps the greatest change was in the status of what is often called 'the average housewife'. During the war, mothers frequently had to be lone parents while fathers were serving abroad. Women found they had managed the problems of running the home, in spite of the dangers of air-raids, and of holding down a responsible job as well. A good proportion of women were happy to relinquish two jobs and return to home-making, but others had become quite fiercely independent and this caused some friction with returning husbands. It also meant that many women had become accustomed to planning meals to accommodate their jobs. The need for Britain to regain our exports meant that there were jobs available for most people who wanted them.

Many new developments for the home, especially the kitchen, were also a help for women wishing to have a job as well as run a home. Electric mixers, liquidizers (blenders) and pressure cookers made the preparation of food easier and cooking quicker. Refrigerators altered shopping habits, for perishable foods could be stored for longer periods. All of these had an effect upon the choice of recipes. Deep freezers were known in America but Britain had to wait a little longer for them.

The years from 1945 onwards were full of changes on the international and national scene. I mention some of the most important of them in the introduction to each year. Britain grieved at the death of the much loved George VI in 1952 but also rejoiced at and were thrilled by the pageantry and splendour of the Coronation of his daughter Elizabeth II in 1953.

The development of television by the BBC meant that many of these events could be seen by the public as they happened. During the war years the radio had given news, information and entertainment but how much greater was the impact of television! As more and more homes had a television set, there was a noticeable effect upon the way evening meals were served and one heard a lot about TV meals served on trays so no time need be spent away from watching the magic screens. Television gradually prevented people going to the cinema or to other outside entertainments as regularly as they once had done.

"My turn to
scrape the dish"

## NOTES ABOUT THE RECIPES

Although many of the recipes in *Marguerite Patten's Post-War Kitchen* are economical, since they are the original ones demonstrated in the years when many foods were still rationed, you will find their flavour is good, for people were much more discerning and critical of dishes after the war ended.

*Ingredients* in the recipes are given in both imperial and metric amounts although, of course, in the years covered by this book metrication was unknown in Britain.

*Oven temperatures* have been carefully tested. If you have a fan oven you will need to reduce the setting slightly when baking cakes and pastry. Consult your manufacturer's handbook.

*Spoon measures* are level in all cases. If the word 'level' is introduced into a recipe it means special care must be taken when filling the spoon.

## THE INGREDIENTS USED

*Eggs* were scarce right up to the time when they were derationed (in 1953) so we used dried eggs a great deal of the time. I have retained reconstituted dried eggs in several recipes for authenticity, but most of my readers will want to use fresh eggs: they are interchangeable in all recipes.

*Flour* for several years after the ending of the war was dark and heavy and needed an excessive amount of baking powder. I have adapted the recipes for use with today's much more refined flour.

I have found it fascinating to recall these important years for this book and I hope that its reader will be equally interested.

*Marguerite Patten*

## RECONSTITUTING DRIED EGG POWDER

One had to be very careful about reconstituting dried eggs during the war. Quite quickly, however, we found that if measurements were accurate, the egg powder made an acceptable substitute. To make one egg, measure one absolutely level tablespoon of dried egg powder. Put it in a cup or basin, then gradually add 2 tablespoons cold water. Stir well until smooth.

# ★1945★

THE CELEBRATIONS THAT marked the ending of the Second World War went on throughout this year; pictures of the street parties and some of the many celebrations will be found in my companion book *The Victory Cookbook.*

It was a great tragedy that American President Roosevelt died in April so could not share in the rejoicings.

The summer of 1945 ended the wartime Coalition Government. A general election brought Labour to power under the leadership of Clement Attlee. Lord Woolton was no longer Minister of Food but his name would long be remembered for his work on the Kitchen Front and also for the dish that bore his name, Woolton Pie, a mixture of seasonal vegetables.

In July of this year the blackout ended amid scenes of great excitement. A well-known song of the war years had a line that read: 'We're going to get lit-up when the lights go on in London' – and no doubt many people did!

No-one expected rationing to be alleviated during 1945, for it was realized that the populations of most of the countries of Europe were starving and their needs must come before those of the British people. Our ships had to bring men and materials back from the various theatres of war, so the transport of any extra food had to take second place. Aid from America, which had helped Britain so much in the previous years, was diverted to the countries previously conquered by Germany and Japan.

The joy felt with the return of many servicemen and women to their homes and the ending of the ever-present fear about hostilities abroad, and attack at home, made rationing almost bearable for most of the population, though there were some rumblings of discontent about the high-handed attitude of shopkeepers, many of whom had lost the habit of wooing customers. People were beginning to feel that the Government must move quickly to make more interesting foods available.

Making preserves of various kinds for the winter months was even more popular than in past years. Many people found they had spare time now that fire-watching and other ARP (Air Raid Precautions) duties were no longer necessary.

Although when the war ended there was no increase in the amount of rationed foods, the kind of recipes I was asked to demonstrate changed quite a lot. Obviously, people were much more relaxed and life lost the terrible feeling of imminent danger. Many people began to invite friends to their home for coffee in the morning or for afternoon tea and wanted recipes for economical home-made biscuits and cakes. I have included some of these recipes in this chapter, as well as a few of the more spartan dishes that would have been served in 1945.

In August of this year it was stated in the press that one million servicemen would be demobilised by December. The same report added that another million people would be released from munition work. The Government urged any men who had worked in the mines to return when possible as it was imperative that Britain increased its coal production.

In November General Charles de Gaulle, who had formed the Free French Forces, was elected to be the new President of France.

☆ ☆ ☆ ☆ ☆ ☆ ☆ ☆ ☆ ☆ ☆ ☆ ☆ ☆ ☆ ☆ ☆ ☆ ☆ ☆ ☆

## BREAKFAST DISHES

Breakfast was still a very important meal in the 1940s and now that nights disturbed by air-raids were over, there was no doubt that young and old were much more wide-awake to enjoy the first meal of the day. Ready-cooked cereals, such as cornflakes, were popular although regular supplies of a specific cereal might be erratic and people had to be content with an alternative. Porridge was served in many homes, for oatmeal and rolled oats were basic foods that were generally in good supply.

The term 'muesli' was not known by the public at this time but, as can be seen in the Food Facts below, the Ministry of Food were suggesting a 'Swiss Breakfast' which was exactly the same thing. The semolina porridge, also below, was not popular.

☆ ☆ ☆ ☆ ☆ ☆ ☆ ☆ ☆ ☆ ☆ ☆ ☆ ☆ ☆ ☆ ☆ ☆ ☆ ☆ ☆ ☆ ☆

## FOOD FACTS

# Using your points for BREAKFAST DISHES

*Savoury Potato Cakes*

WHAT to give the men-folk and the children for breakfast is a problem in many households. A small, well-planned outlay of points will help you to give the family a good hot meal for starting off the day. The recipes here are kitchen-tested.

**Swiss Breakfast *(for 4)***
*4 oz. barley flakes or kernels; 4 tablesps. milk; ½ lb. grated apple; 1-2 level tablesps. sugar.*
Soak the barley flakes or kernels overnight in barely enough water to cover. In the morning, beat up well with the other ingredients. This is a delicious change from porridge.

**Savoury Potato Cakes *(for 4)***
*1 lb. left-over mashed potato; 1 tin sardines (4½ oz. size); 2 level tablesps. chopped parsley; 1 level teasp. salt; ¼ level teasp. pepper.*
Mix all ingredients well together. Turn on to a board and shape into 8 cakes. Brown under grill on both sides, or bake in a moderate oven till firm and brown.

**Semolina Porridge *(for 4)*** *4-6 oz. semolina; 2 level teaspoons salt; 2 pints liquid (1 pint or less milk, and remainder in water).*
Blend the semolina and salt with a little of the cold liquid. Bring the remainder to the boil and pour on to the blended semolina. Return to the pan and boil gently for 15-20 minutes, stirring well to prevent it burning. (If thick porridge is preferred use the larger amount of semolina.)

**Fried Pilchards on Fried Bread *(for 4)*** *1 tin pilchards, 15-oz. size; 4 slices of bread; fat for frying if necessary.*
Fry the pilchards till brown on both sides. They should be sufficiently oily to fry without extra fat. Remove from the pan and keep hot. Add a little extra fat if necessary, to fry the slices of bread till golden brown on both sides. Divide the pilchards on to the 4 slices of fried bread and serve hot.

**CUT THIS OUT AND KEEP IT**

ISSUED BY THE MINISTRY OF FOOD, LONDON, S.W.I. FOOD FACTS No. 331

## Breakfast Quickies

The bacon ration was small and people were always trying to find ways to make it go further, for bacon was still a favourite breakfast food. Where quantities are given the dish gives 4 helpings.

**Bacon Fritters**: These are a good way to eke out a small amount of bacon. Fry 2 bacon rashers then cut into small pieces. Make a batter with 2 oz (50 g) self-raising flour, a pinch of salt, 1 reconstituted dried egg (page 10) or a fresh egg and 5 tablespoons milk or milk and water. Add the bacon and season to taste.

Drop spoonfuls into a little hot fat and fry until crisp and brown on either side.

**Cheese Fritters**: Follow the recipe for Bacon Fritters above but use grated cheese instead of bacon. These are excellent with cooked tomatoes.

**Herring Roes**: Coat soft or hard herring roes with a little seasoned flour, and fry in hot fat. If no fat is available for frying, put the roes on a plate with a tablespoon or two of milk and seasoning. Cover and steam for 10 minutes. Serve on hot toast.

**Kippers**: These can be grilled, fried or steamed but the easiest method of cooking is to put them in a large dish, pour over boiling water, cover the dish and leave for 5 minutes.

**Kipper Scramble**: To make 1 or 2 kippers go further, flake the cooked flesh from the skin and bones. Mix the flesh with 2 or 3 reconstituted dried eggs (page 10) or fresh eggs. Season lightly. Heat 1 oz (25 g) margarine in a pan, pour in the egg mixture and scramble lightly.

The flesh from cooked bloaters, smoked haddock or white fish could be used instead.

## EGGY BREAD

*Preparation time: 5 minutes*
*Cooking time: 4 minutes*
*Quantity: 4 helpings*

This was a good way of making 2 eggs serve 4 people. It appealed very much to children, particularly those who were not over-fond of a whole boiled or fried egg. This is the original recipe, using reconstituted dried eggs (see page 10), but you could use fresh eggs instead. Remember to reconstitute the dried eggs carefully, making sure there are no lumps.

2 level tablespoons dried egg
    powder
4 tablespoons water
salt and pepper
4 large slices bread
1 oz (25 g) fat

Reconstitute the egg powder with the water (page 10) and add seasoning to taste. Pour on to a flat dish.

Dip the slices of bread in the egg until well coated, making sure all the egg is used. Do not leave the bread soaking for too long for this makes it soggy and inclined to break.

Melt the fat in a large frying pan and cook the coated bread until golden on both sides and the egg is firmly set. Serve at once.

FOOD ✪ FACTS

## WHERE THERE'S FISH THERE'S A GOOD . . . BREAKFAST

**W**IN top marks as a housewife by giving your family a substantial breakfast. Not easy — but it can be done if you plan ahead and make good use of fish. Here are some breakfast dishes. Some are very quick, the others can be made the day before and served in a jiffy.

### FISH PASTY

**Ingredients:** 6 oz. short-crust pastry, 8 oz. cooked fish, 8 oz. mixed cooked vegetables, 2 tablespoons chopped parsley, salt and pepper, ¼ pint white sauce, 1 tablespoon vinegar.

**Method:** Roll out the pastry thinly, cut into rounds about 6 in. in diameter, flake the fish, mix it with the other ingredients and season well. Put a portion of mixture in half of each circle of pastry. Fold over the remaining half of pastry, seal the edges and bake in a moderate oven for about 25 to 30 minutes.

### GRILLED HERRINGS

*(Suitable for whole or boned fish)*

If the fish is to be grilled whole, cut the flesh in three or four places across the back. Season the fish well. Put a knob or two of margarine or dripping on the fish. Place under a hot grill and cook till brown on both sides. Eat these plain or, if you like, serve with a mustard or tomato sauce.

### FISH ROES

1. **Hard Roes:** Remove from herrings, wash, and boil gently until tender. This takes about 15 minutes. Season and serve with a knob of margarine on toast.

2. **Soft Roes:** Wash the roes and place in a frying-pan with just enough liquid (milk and water) to cover bottom of pan. Add a small knob of margarine and season with pepper and salt. Cook slowly for 10-15 minutes and serve on toast.

**CUT THIS OUT AND KEEP IT**

THE MINISTRY OF FOOD, LONDON, S.W.I.     FOOD FACTS No. 381

## BACON AND POTATO CAKES

*Preparation time: 10 minutes*
*Cooking time: 8 minutes*
*Quantity: 4 helpings*

This was a good way of making 1 or 2 bacon rashers go a long way. They added flavour to the potato cakes. The rinds would be fried until very crisp then broken into small pieces and added to the mixture or saved for a garnish on soups or stews.

The Ministry of Food advisers always stressed 'cook extra potatoes to use in savoury or sweet dishes'. The timings for this recipe depend upon the potatoes being ready cooked.

1 or 2 bacon rashers, derinded
12 oz (350 g) cooked potatoes
1–2 tablespoons milk
1 tablespoon chopped parsley
salt and pepper
1 tablespoon flour
little fat, if necessary

Fry the bacon rashers and rinds until very crisp, and chop into small pieces. Mash the potatoes and add enough milk to make a fairly firm mixture with the bacon, parsley and seasoning. Form into 4 large or 8 small round cakes. Lightly coat the cakes in the flour then fry them until crisp and brown on both sides in the bacon fat remaining in the pan. If there is very little then melt a small knob of cooking fat in the pan before adding the cakes.

Serve with cooked halved tomatoes or a few heated bottled tomatoes.

## MAIN MEALS

In the days of air-raids many families had their main meal in the middle of the day, for the evenings and nights could be very disturbed. Now that there was no fear of unwelcome interruptions people could enjoy an evening meal if they so wished. These are some of the popular dishes of 1945.

### CURRIED VEGETABLE SOUP

*Preparation time: 25 minutes*
*Cooking time: 12–22 minutes (see method)*
*Quantity: 4 helpings*

Root vegetables were a staple part of the British diet during the whole year. Raw carrots and turnips became part of vegetable salads. Onions were scarce during the winter months but became more readily available out of season after the war ended. Much work had been done by the Ministry of Food to educate the public to the fact that cooking vegetables for the minimum time retained the maximum amount of vitamins and mineral salts as well as flavour and texture.

2 medium carrots
1 small turnip
1 small parsnip
2 onions
2 potatoes
2 tomatoes
1 oz (25 g) margarine or cooking fat
1 tablespoon flour
2 teaspoons curry powder,
   or to taste
1¼ pints (750 ml) water
salt and pepper
¼ pint (150 ml) milk

Peel the vegetables. The tomatoes should be skinned. For speedy cooking, grate the vegetables coarsely; otherwise cut them in small neat dice. Chop the tomatoes. Melt the fat in a saucepan, add the onions and cook gently for 5 minutes then stir in the flour and curry powder. Add the water, bring to the boil then put in the remaining ingredients except the tomatoes and milk. Cook for 10 minutes if the vegetables are grated or for 15–20 minutes if cut into dice. Add the tomatoes and milk and heat for a few minutes.

### CUCUMBER SOUP

*Preparation time: 10 minutes*
*Cooking time: 15 minutes*
*Quantity: 4 helpings*

'Dig for Victory' had been a slogan throughout the war years so a large percentage of the population had become good at growing vegetables. Home-grown cucumbers were highly prized.

1 medium cucumber
1 oz (25 g) margarine
1 medium onion or bunch spring onions,
   finely chopped
1 pint (600 ml) water
salt and pepper
2 teaspoons finely chopped mint
½ pint (300 ml) milk

It is better to remove most of the peel from the cucumber as it gives a very bitter taste to the soup. You can leave on about ½–1 inch (1.25–2.5 cm) to add to the colour of the soup. Dice or grate the cucumber pulp, and finely chop the small amount of skin. Heat the margarine in a saucepan, add the onion(s) and cook gently for 5 minutes. Add the water, bring to the boil then put in the cucumber, seasoning and mint. Simmer for 8 minutes then add the milk and heat for 2 minutes.

#### VARIATIONS
The soup can be rubbed through a sieve.
Use unsweetened evaporated milk instead of the ordinary milk.

#### MODERN TOUCHES
Use single cream instead of milk.
Liquidize the soup.

**DAILY EXPRESS**
WEDNESDAY AUGUST 15 1945
One Penny
*Attlee, at midnight, gives news that it is all over*

# PEACE ON EARTH

### JAPS REPLY: We have the honour to surrender.
### Mikado orders all his Forces to cease fire

**TERMS ACCEPTED—AND NO CONDITIONS**

*MacArthur gets ready to move in*

PASTE THIS ON YOUR WINDOW!

HARA-KIRI EVE IN JAPAN
**Tears flow at Sublime Palace**

PETAIN TO DIE

People get out of bed

TODAY AND TOMORROW ARE VJ HOLIDAYS

# FOOD FACTS

## WHAT TO HAVE FOR SUPPER?

*HERRINGS are just about the tastiest fish you can get!*

## HERRINGS AMERICAINE

*Preparation time: 15 minutes*
*Cooking time: 25 minutes*
*Quantity: 4 helpings*

There was a spate of recipes using the term 'Americaine' when the war ended, for America had been our good friend and ally. Greaseproof paper was almost unobtainable, so the wrappings of margarine and other fats were carefully hoarded.

**For the stuffing:**
1 oz (25 g) margarine
1 medium onion, grated
    or finely chopped
2 medium tomatoes,
    chopped
2 oz (50 g) soft breadcrumbs
1 tablespoon chopped parsley
1 reconstituted dried egg
    (see page 10) or fresh egg

salt and pepper

**To cook the herrings:**
4 herrings, heads removed
    and boned
½ tablespoon margarine,
    melted

Heat the margarine for the stuffing, add the onion and cook for 5 minutes. Mix in the other stuffing ingredients. Put the stuffing into the herrings and place in a baking dish. Top with the half tablespoon melted margarine. Cover the dish with a lid or with margarine paper. Bake for 25 minutes in a preheated oven set to 190°C (375°F), Gas Mark 5. Serve hot or cold with vegetables or salad.

## SAUSAGES IN CIDER

*Preparation time: 5 minutes*
*Cooking time: 20 or 35 minutes*
*(see method)*
*Quantity: 4 helpings*

The sausages obtainable during this period of the 1940s were singularly lacking in meat and flavour and often difficult to obtain, so it meant a queue at the butcher's. Sausages were unrationed, so gave another main dish. This was a good way to impart some taste to them.

1 lb (450 g) sausages
1 oz (25 g) cooking fat
    or margarine
1 onion, thinly sliced
2 dessert apples, cored and sliced
½ pint (300 ml) cider
salt and pepper

Prick the sausages. Melt the fat in a frying pan then add the sausages and cook steadily for 5 minutes, turning them so they brown on all sides. Stir in the onion and cook for 2 minutes then add the rest of the ingredients. Cover the pan and simmer for a good 10 minutes. Serve with mashed potatoes and cabbage.

If more convenient, brown the sausges in the frying pan, add the onions, as above, then transfer to a casserole. Heat the apples with the cider in the frying pan then spoon over the sausages. Cover the dish and bake for 25 minutes in a preheated oven set to 190°C (375°F), Gas Mark 5.

## CHEESE AND TOMATO CHARLOTTE

*Preparation time: 15 minutes*
*Cooking time: 30 minutes*
*Quantity: 4 helpings*

This recipe is a good way of using up various rather hard pieces of cheese.

4 large slices bread
2 oz (50 g) cooking fat or
    dripping (see Variations, right)
1 pint (600 ml) jar bottled
    tomatoes
6 oz (175 g) cheese, grated
1 medium onion, finely
    chopped or grated
1 tablespoon chopped parsley
salt and pepper

**For the sauce:**
liquid from tomatoes
water (see method)
1 level tablespoon cornflour
1 tablespoon chopped chives
1 tablespoon chopped parsley
1 teaspoon made mustard
few drops Worcestershire sauce

Cut the bread into neat fingers of uniform size. Melt the fat or dripping in a frying pan and fry the bread until brown and crisp on both sides.

Drain the tomatoes, retaining the liquid. Mix the tomatoes with the cheese, onion, parsley and seasoning.

Preheat the oven to 190°C (375°F), Gas Mark 5. Put half the bread into a pie dish or casserole. Top

with the cheese and tomato mixture then the rest of the fried bread. Bake for 20–25 minutes.

Meanwhile, make the sauce. Measure the tomato liquid and add enough water to make up to ½ pint (300 ml). Blend with the cornflour. Pour into a saucepan and stir over a medium heat until thickened. Add the herbs, mustard, Worcestershire sauce and any extra seasoning required. Serve the sauce separately.

**VARIATIONS**

If short of fat or dripping, crisp the bread in the oven before making this dish. Use fresh tomatoes instead of bottled ones. Cook until tender then strain and continue as in the recipe.

## SUMMER BEETROOT SOUP

*Preparation time: 15 minutes*
*Cooking time: 10 minutes*
*Quantity: 4 helpings*

This soup is particularly good when young cooked beetroot are available. Yeast extract (Marmite) was used to add flavour to many dishes for this was often available in 1945.

> about 10 oz (300 g) cooked beetroot, peeled and grated or finely chopped
> bunch spring onions, chopped
> 1½ pints (900 ml) water
> ½ teaspoon Marmite, or to taste
> salt and pepper
> 1 teaspoon vinegar

Put all the ingredients into a saucepan, being sparing with the salt for the yeast extract is salty. Simmer for 10 minutes.

**VARIATION**
Omit the Marmite and use a stock cube instead.

**A MODERN TOUCH**
Serve the soup topped with yogurt.

## TRIPE MORNAY

*Preparation time: 20 minutes*
*Cooking time: 1 hour*
*Quantity: 4 helpings*

Tripe has always been an acquired taste in Britain, and is more popular in the north of England than in the south. It was unrationed meat, so many people would seize the opportunity to buy it on the rare occasions it was available.

> 1 lb (450 g) tripe
> water (see method)
> 2 medium onions,
>     thinly sliced
> salt and pepper
> few drops vinegar

**For the sauce:**
> 1 oz (25 g) margarine
> 1 oz (25 g) plain flour
> ¼ pint (150 ml) milk
> 2 oz (50 g) cheese, grated

Wash the tripe in plenty of cold water then cut into neat 2 inch (5 cm) squares. Put into a saucepan; cover with cold water. Bring the water to the boil, strain the tripe and discard the liquid. This is 'blanching' the meat, to give it a better colour and flavour.

Place the tripe and onions in a saucepan, add just enough water to cover, a little seasoning and the vinegar. Cover the pan and simmer for 4–5 minutes. Strain the tripe and onions, retaining 7 fl oz (200 ml) of the liquid from the pan.

In a separate pan, heat the margarine for the sauce, stir in the flour, then the milk. Bring to the boil and cook until thickened. Spoon the tripe, onions and reserved liquid into the thick sauce. Heat gently then stir in the cheese and adjust the seasoning. Serve with creamed potatoes and mixed cooked root vegetables.

**VARIATIONS**
**Tripe au Gratin:** Spoon the tripe mixture into a flameproof dish and top with a little grated cheese and soft breadcrumbs. Place under a preheated grill or in a moderately hot oven until the top is crisp and golden brown.

## WILTSHIRE MEAT CAKES

*Preparation time: 10 minutes*
*Cooking time: 15 minutes*
*Quantity: 4 helpings*

These were a favourite summer dish when home-grown tomatoes were available. Bottled tomatoes were rather too moist.

> 2 large tomatoes, skinned
>     and chopped
> 8 oz (225 g) minced beef
> 8 oz (225 g) sausagemeat
> ½ teaspoon paprika
> 1 oz (25 g) soft breadcrumbs
> 1 tablespoon chopped parsley
> 1 egg
> salt and pepper

**For frying:**
> 1 oz (25 g) dripping or fat

Mix the tomatoes with all the other ingredients. Form into 8 small round fairly flat cakes. Heat the dripping or fat in a large frying pan. Cook the cakes rapidly for 2 minutes on either side then lower the heat and cook steadily for 11 minutes. Serve with creamed potatoes and a green vegetable or cold with a salad.

# FOOD FACTS

**PUDDINGS & POINTS**

**Let's** use some of our points to solve the pudding problem. For some men and most children it's the "afters" that make the meal.

## GINGER RHUBARB CRISP

*Preparation time: 20 minutes*
*Cooking time: 30 minutes*
*Quantity: 4 helpings*

1 lb (450 g) rhubarb,
   trimmed weight
2 oz (50 g) cooking
   dates, chopped
2 oz (50 g) sugar,
   preferably Demerara
2 tablespoons water

**For the topping:**
2 oz (50 g) margarine
1 oz (25 g) sugar,
   preferably granulated
1 tablespoon golden syrup
1–2 teaspoons ground ginger,
   or to taste
4 oz (115 g) rolled oats

Cut the rhubarb into 1½ inch (3.75 cm) lengths and put into a pie dish with the dates, sugar and water.

For the topping, melt the margarine with the sugar and syrup in a saucepan. Stir in the ginger and rolled oats. Mix thoroughly then spoon over the rhubarb; spread flat with a damp (not wet) knife. Make sure all the fruit is covered.

Bake in a preheated oven set to 180°C (350°F), Gas Mark 4 for 30 minutes.

### VARIATIONS
Use cooking apples instead of rhubarb. In this case, precook the apples for 10 minutes before adding the topping.

Other fruits can be used when in season. Soft fruits do not need precooking before adding the topping.

## NORFOLK PUDDING

*Preparation time: 15 minutes*
*Cooking time: 40 minutes*
*Quantity: 4–6 helpings*

**For the batter:**
4 oz (115 g) plain flour
pinch salt
1 level tablespoon dried egg
   powder with 2 tablespoons
   water or 1 fresh egg
½ pint (scant 300 ml) milk
   or milk and water

**For the fruit base:**
½ oz (15 g) fat
1 lb (450 g) cooking apples
2 tablespoons dried fruit,
   if available
2 oz (50 g) sugar

**For the topping:**
little sugar

For the batter, sift the flour with the salt and dried egg powder then add the rest of the liquid and beat until a smooth batter. If using a fresh egg, add it to the sifted flour and salt.

Preheat the oven to 220°C (425°F), Gas Mark 7. Put the fat into a large pie dish or casserole and heat for a few minutes in the oven. Peel, core and thinly slice the apples, add to the hot fat with the dried fruit and sugar. Mix well, cover the dish and return to the oven for 5 minutes. Uncover the dish, pour the batter over the fruit and bake for 25–30 minutes, or until well-risen and brown. Top with sugar and serve at once.

## GYPSY TART

*Preparation time: 25 minutes*
*Cooking time: 35–40 minutes*
*Quantity: 4–6 helpings*

There are several different recipes for this tart. This is the one made when rationing was still in force in 1945. Evaporated milk was highly prized. It was obtainable on the points system (the system under which rationing was controlled; everyone had an allowance of 16 points a month).

**For the shortcrust pastry:**
6 oz (175 g) plain flour
pinch salt
3 oz (85 g) fat
water, to bind

**For the filling:**
1 oz (25 g) butter or margarine
2 oz (50 g) sugar,
   preferably Demerara
1 level tablespoon golden syrup
1 egg
¼ pint (150 ml) evaporated milk

For the pastry, sift the flour and salt into a bowl, rub in the fat and add sufficient water to make a dough with a firm rolling consistency. Roll out and use to line an 8 inch (20 cm) flan tin or ring on an upturned baking tray.

Preheat the oven to 200°C (400°F), Gas Mark 6 and bake the pastry blind (See Apricot and Lemon Flan, page 47) for 15 minutes. Take the pastry shell out of the oven and lower the oven temperature to 160°C (325°F), Gas Mark 3.

While the pastry is cooking, prepare the filling. Cream the butter or margarine with the sugar and syrup. Beat the egg and add to the creamed mixture then slowly stir in the evaporated milk. Spoon into the partially baked pastry case, return to the oven and bake for a further 20–25 minutes, or until the filling is firm. Serve cold.

# ★1946★

**D**URING THIS YEAR **rationing became more stringent again. Even children were affected when the sweet ration, normally l2 oz (350 g) a month, was halved. There were cuts in the meagre allowances of some other foods and in July bread was put on ration. This caused a great uproar, for at no time during the war had this happened.**

There were queues at bakers' shops and one heard more about the British Housewives League. This was formed by angry women who felt that the Government was not doing enough to improve the quantity and variety of foods available. Other women's organizations joined in the protests and so did building, foundry and farm workers. Their protests arose from the fact that the miners' meat ration was increased but not those of other people doing heavy work.

Fuel supplies were bad and fuel cuts were quite normal. This made cooking meals even more challenging.

In spite of all the problems, the food manufacturer, Bird's Eye, produced a frozen food that would be popular for many decades to come. I was asked to present their frozen Fish Fingers to the media at a hotel in London. The company also planted their first peas in l946, though it would be several years before they were ready to be frozen and sold to the public.

An important radio programme was launched in October l946. This was *Woman's Hour* which was, interestingly enough, at first compèred by a man.

An even more exciting event was the restart of BBC Television. There had been experimental transmissions before the war but now the BBC were launching their programmes for the future. The hours of viewing were severely limited.

The very few members of the public who were fortunate enough to view television were fascinated to see ballet and plays and some cooking. The cookery programmes were given by Philip Harben.

The good food news was that small supplies of imported fruits were coming into the country. Bananas were among the first of these. Adults, who remembered this fruit with delight, promised their children a great treat when they tasted their first banana. Not all children were enthusiastic, particularly if they tried to eat the fruit with the skin on, as happened from time to time. Dried bananas also began to make an appearance about this time. Clementines were imported for the first time. Whale meat, a food Britain was to hear more about in the coming year or so, was served at a special luncheon in London. Poultry, which had been almost unobtainable for town-dwellers during the war years, became more available but the price was increased to an unbelievably high 5s 4d (over 25 p) per 1 lb (450 g).

Many of the chickens available were elderly boiling fowls, who had given good service in laying eggs, and now that time had ended they were killed and sold as boiling fowls. These needed prolonged cooking to make them tender. The good thing was their bodies contained a good deal of natural fat. This meant that if the birds were simmered (not boiled as the name suggests) you obtained good tasting tender chicken, plus excellent stock with a thin layer of precious fat on top which could be used in cooking.

## SAUSAGE SAVOURY BALLS

*Preparation time: 15 minutes*
*Cooking time: 15 minutes*
*Quantity: 8 balls*

These make a good cold dish to take on a picnic, or they can be served hot with mixed vegetables.

1 oz (25 g) cooking fat
1 medium onion, finely chopped
1 small dessert apple, peeled, cored and grated
12 oz (350 g) sausagemeat
2 oz (50 g) soft breadcrumbs

**For the coating:**
little milk or beaten egg
1–1½ oz (25–40 g) crisp breadcrumbs

**For frying:**
1–2 oz (25–50 g) dripping

Melt the fat in a pan, add the onion and cook for 5 minutes, taking care it does not brown. Blend with all the other ingredients and form into 8 balls. Coat the balls with milk or egg then roll them in crisp breadcrumbs.

Melt the dripping for frying in the pan until hot and fry the sausage balls quickly until brown on all sides. Lower the heat and cook for a further 10 minutes.

### VARIATION

If bread is scarce, omit the crumbs in the mixture and use the same weight of mashed potato. Simply coat the balls in seasoned flour instead of the crisp breadcrumbs. In this case, the milk or egg is not necessary.

## BEEF AND PRUNE HOTPOT

*Preparation time: 25 minutes, plus soaking time for prunes*
*Cooking time: 2 hours*
*Quantity: 4 helpings*

As fuel cuts were usual during 1946, dishes like this would be cooked whenever fuel was available and reheated as required. I remember being asked to warn people on *Woman's Hour* that meat dishes like this must be thoroughly reheated before serving. Onions were not plentiful during the winter months and leeks were often substituted, although the severe frosts at the end of 1946 made even these difficult to buy.

4 oz (115 g) prunes
water
little Marmite or ½ stock cube
8–12 oz (225–350 g) stewing beef
1¼–1½ lb (550–675 g) potatoes, thinly sliced
2 onions or 3 leeks, thinly sliced
salt and pepper
1 oz (25 g) margarine

Put the prunes into a container, cover with plenty of water and leave to soak for at least 12 hours. Strain the prunes but save ¼ pint (150 ml) of the water, adding a very little Marmite or the stock cube to it to give more flavour. Cut the beef into thin strips.

Arrange a layer of potatoes and onions or leeks in a casserole; season lightly. Add the meat and prunes, then the rest of the onions or leeks with more seasoning. End with a neat covering of potatoes. Pour the prune liquid over the ingredients. Top with small dabs of margarine. Do not cover the casserole at this stage, as the lid could stick to the margarine.

Put the casserole into a preheated oven set to 160°C (325°F), Gas Mark 3 and heat for 15 minutes, then put on the lid and cook for a further 1½ hours. Remove the lid for the final 15 minutes so the potatoes brown slightly.

## PLUM DUMPLINGS

*Preparation time: 25 minutes*
*Cooking time: 25 minutes*
*Quantity: 4 helpings*

These satisfying dumplings were really very delicious. The plums should be just ripe, but firm enough to split. The plums should not be too large for the amount of pastry given.

8 plums
4 teaspoons plum jam
water (see method)

**For the dumplings:**
8 oz (225 g) self-raising flour or plain flour with 2 teaspoons baking powder
pinch salt
2 oz (50 g) shredded suet or margarine
1 oz (25 g) sugar
water, to bind

**For the coating:**
little sugar

Halve the plums, carefully remove the stones then sandwich the halves together with the jam. Bring about 2 pints (1.2 litres) of water to the boil in a large saucepan.

For the dumplings, sift the flour, or flour and baking powder, and the salt into a bowl, add the suet or rub in the margarine. Stir in the sugar and then gradually add sufficient water to make a mixture with a soft rolling consistency. Roll out to about ¼ inch (6 mm) thick then cut into 8 portions. Moisten the edges of each portion of dough with water and wrap around the plums; seal the joins firmly.

Drop the dumplings into the boiling water, allowing the water to boil briskly for at least 8 minutes so the pastry rises, then lower the heat to a steady simmer for about 17 minutes. When cooked, remove the dumplings from the water with a perforated spoon or fish slice. Dust with sugar and serve hot.

## CARROT AND POTATO CHOWDER

*Preparation time: 25 minutes*
*Cooking time: 25–30 minutes*
*Quantity: 4 helpings*

Many people had learned quite a lot of American recipes from meeting service men and women from the USA. Chowder, a very thick and satisfying American soup, was ideal for the extreme cold of the winter of 1946.

> 1 lb (450 g) potatoes
> 12 oz (350 g) carrots
> 2 large onions
> 2 bacon rashers
>   (optional)
> 1 oz (25 g) cooking fat
>   or margarine
> ³/₄ pint (450 ml) water
> salt and pepper
> 1–2 teaspoons mustard
>   powder
> ½ pint (300 ml) milk
> 2 tablespoons chopped
>   parsley or watercress
>   leaves

Peel the vegetables then cut the potatoes and carrots into neat dice about ⅓ inch (8 mm) in size; do not make them smaller, as they would break in cooking. The onions can be finely chopped. Remove the rinds from the bacon and dice the rashers.

Melt the fat or margarine and the bacon rinds, add the onions and cook gently for 5 minutes. Remove the bacon rinds and add the diced bacon; cook for a few more minutes then pour in the water. Bring to the boil, add a little seasoning and the carrots. Cook for 5 minutes then put in the potatoes. Continue cooking slowly for 15 minutes, watching the vegetables to ensure they do not break. Blend the mustard powder with the milk, add to the soup and heat through.

Top with the parsley or watercress just before serving.

### VARIATION

Use a mixture of vegetables instead of just the carrots, onions and potatoes.

## WOMAN'S HOUR

The start of *Woman's Hour* roused enormous interest and the programme had very high listening figures. I was asked to take part in the programme on its second day and not only gave a recipe for a seasonal stew but also had to answer questions on the air about sponges and baked custards from cooks who were listening to the programme: surprisingly, these were male cooks from the Royal Navy! Even at the beginning of its life *Woman's Hour* appealed to men as well as women.

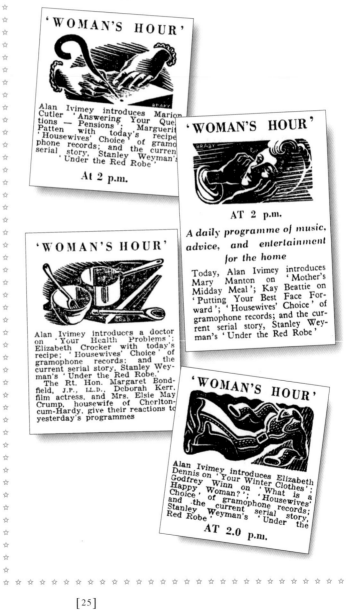

## 'Television is Here Again'

Tomorrow afternoon the BBC Television Service resumes its daily transmission from the Alexandra Palace after an interval of more than six years. Before the war the Alexandra Palace station led the world in television, and, on the eve of the reopening, this programme explains how a television service is run, recalls what pre-war television was like in Britain, and outlines what viewers will see in the coming months. Written by Robert Barr. Produced by John Glyn - Jones. Tonight at 9.30

G. M. GARRO-JONES, M.P., Chairman of the Television Advisory Committee, who broadcasts at 9.15

## SAVOURY BREAST OF MUTTON

*Preparation time: 25 minutes*
*Cooking time: 1¼–2 hours*
*Quantity: 4 helpings*

Mutton was still available in 1946. Today, one could substitute 2 smaller breasts of lamb in this recipe and shorten the cooking time to 1¼–1½ hours. Any fat left after cooking the meat would be carefully saved.

1 large breast of mutton

**For the stuffing:**
1 large cooking apple, peeled, cored and finely diced
1 medium leek, thinly sliced
8 oz (225 g) sausagemeat
2 tablespoons chopped parsley
1 teaspoon chopped mint
½ teaspoon chopped thyme
salt and pepper

Cut away the bones from the meat (use them to make a good stock).
 Blend all the ingredients for the stuffing together. Spread over the breast and roll up firmly. Tie with string. Put into a preheated oven set to 160°C (325°F), Gas Mark 3 and cook until tender. Serve with jacket potatoes and green vegetables.

## DAILY SERIAL

Dick Barton begins his career as a special agent this evening at 6.45. You can follow his adventures at the same time every day from—

**MONDAY TO FRIDAY**

## CHESTNUT CREAMS

*Preparation time: 25 minutes*
*Cooking time: 30 minutes*
*Quantity: 4–6 helpings*

My memory of hot chestnuts goes back to 1946–1947 when we had a terribly cold winter that lasted for many weeks. A man had a barrow with a stove on from which he sold roasted chestnuts just outside Harrods, where I was working. I used to buy a bag of these several times a week. They warmed my hands as I sat in the train and ate them. Chestnuts were on sale that winter and this dessert was a great favourite in my home.

1 lb (450 g) chestnuts
1 teaspoon vanilla essence
3 tablespoons apricot jam
2 tablespoons water
1 oz (25 g) sugar
7½ fl oz (250 ml) unsweetened evaporated milk (whipped as page 59)

Wash the chestnuts then slit the skins on the rounded side in the shape of a cross. Put into boiling water, boil steadily for 10 minutes then remove from the water and take off the outer shells and inner brown skins while still warm. Put the chestnuts into enough boiling water to cover, add the vanilla essence and simmer for 10–15 minutes, or until soft. Sieve or mash most of the nuts, saving 2 or 3 for decoration.
 Heat the jam with the water and sugar, add the chestnut purée and blend well. Leave until quite cold. Fold into the whipped evaporated milk and spoon into glasses. Top with halved nuts.

### A MODERN TOUCH
Use unsweetened canned chestnut purée and whipped cream.

*"Don't talk to me about Food . . .*

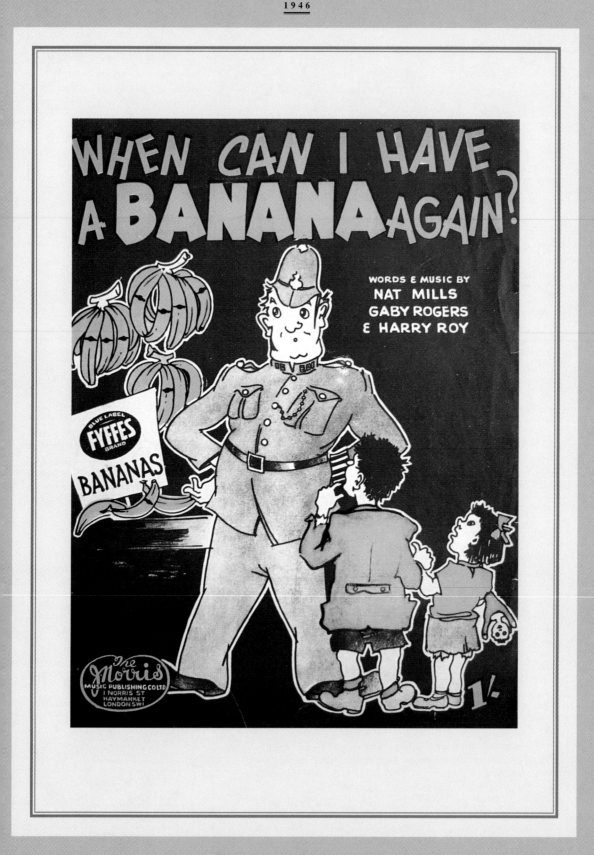

## HOME-MADE BREAD

*Preparation time: 30 minutes, plus time for proving*
*Cooking time: 40 minutes*
*Quantity: 2 loaves*

When bread became rationed, many people who had never attempted to make bread before, bought yeast and started to bake. Fresh yeast was difficult to obtain but tins of dried yeast were available. The method used here is for fresh or dried yeast; see the 'modern touch' at the end of the recipe for a note about using quick-acting yeast.

1½ lb (675 g) plain flour
½ teaspoon salt
¾ pint (450 ml) water
½ oz (15 g) fresh yeast or
2 teaspoons dried yeast
with 1 teaspoon sugar

Sift the flour and salt into a mixing bowl. Heat the water until just warm.

If using fresh yeast, cream it then add the water and leave until the surface is frothy. If using dried yeast, add it with the sugar to the water, top with a sprinkling of the flour and leave until frothy. This takes 12–15 minutes.

Make a well in the centre of the flour, pour in the yeast liquid and mix well. Turn out on to a floured board and knead. Use the heel of your hand (base of the palm) with a pulling and stretching movement. You can tell if the dough is sufficiently kneaded by firmly pressing it with a finger. If the impression comes out then the dough is ready for the next stage. If it stays in then continue to knead and test again.

When sufficiently kneaded, shape the dough into a ball and return to the bowl. Cover with a cloth and leave in a warm place to prove (rise) until double the original size. In an airing cupboard it will take about 1 hour; if left at room temperature, it will take about 2 hours.

Turn the dough on to a floured surface and knead again (this process is known as 'knocking back').

Form the dough into 2 round loaves and place on a baking tray to prove again until almost twice the original size. Cover it very lightly with a cloth. This stage will take about 45–60 minutes at room temperature.

Meanwhile, preheat the oven to 220°C (425°F), Gas Mark 7. Bake the bread for 35–40 minutes. To test if the loaves are baked, remove them from the tray and tap the base. They should sound hollow.

### VARIATIONS

If you want to use only 1 lb (450 g) flour, use ½ pint (300 ml) water but the same amount of yeast. Reduce the salt slightly.

If you use 3 lb (1.35 kg) flour, use double the amount of fresh or dried yeast.

Rub about 1 oz (25 g) cooking fat or lard or margarine into the flour and salt. This gives a more moist bread.

### A MODERN TOUCH

Use strong instead of plain flour. This was not on sale in 1946.

Use the modern quick-acting yeast which can be mixed with the flour. Follow the packet instructions.

## MORE KINDS OF BREAD

Having made ordinary bread, you can vary it in many ways. When more ingredients became available, rather more elaborate breads were made. The following recipes are based on the Home-made Bread, left:

**Cheese Bread:** Add 2 oz (50 g) finely grated cheese to the flour. Flavour the flour with a good shake of pepper and a pinch of mustard powder as well as the salt.

**Fruit Bread:** Add 2–3 oz (50–85 g) dried fruit to the flour. ½–1 teaspoon allspice can be sifted with the flour.

**Herb Bread:** Add 2 tablespoons chopped parsley and 1 tablespoon chopped chives to the flour.

**Malt Bread:** Add 2 tablespoons malt extract to the other ingredients. This bread is better mixed with milk, or milk and water, rather than all water. If using liquid malt (rather like a thick syrup), you will need slightly less liquid than given in the recipe. If using powdered malt or Ovaltine (a good source of malt), use the same amount of liquid as in the basic recipe.

**Rolls:** Make the bread dough; when it has been proved, divide it into about 18 portions and form into rounds or the desired shapes. Put on baking trays and allow to prove again for about 25 minutes. Bake in a preheated oven set to 230°C (450°F), Gas Mark 8 for 12–15 minutes.

NO MORE RATION CUTS
WOMEN OF BAYSWATER
AND PADDINGTON!
COME AND SIGN THE
PROTEST TO THE MINISTER OF FOOD
AGAINST FURTHER CUTS IN
OUR RATIONS.

## BAKING POWDER ROLLS

*Preparation time: 5 minutes*
*Cooking time: 12–15 minutes*
*Quantity: 8–10 rolls*

These were often made during the time of bread rationing. The basic recipe here can be varied by adding chopped parsley, or other herbs, for a savoury roll or a tablespoon of sugar to make a sweet roll.

8 oz (225 g) self-raising flour
    or plain flour with 2 teaspoons
    baking powder
good pinch salt
1/2–1 oz (15–25 g) margarine
milk, or milk and water, to mix

Preheat the oven to 220°C (425°F), Gas Mark 7. Sift the flour, or flour and baking powder, and the salt into a bowl. Rub in the margarine and blend with the milk, or milk and water, to a soft dough. Take off small pieces and form into rolls or finger shapes. Place on an ungreased baking tray and cook for 12–15 minutes. Eat when fresh.

☆ ☆ ☆ ☆ ☆ ☆ ☆ ☆ ☆ ☆ ☆ ☆ ☆ ☆ ☆ ☆ ☆ ☆ ☆ ☆ ☆ ☆ ☆ ☆

## SWISS BUNS

People who had never used yeast before became very enthusiastic about their home baking. They realised that if they had hungry children yeast buns could be made with little or no fat. These buns are based on the Home-made Bread dough (see page 28).
To make 7 or 8 Swiss Buns, take off about a quarter of the yeast dough after it has proved. Form into finger shapes 4 inches (10 cm) long and put on to baking trays, leaving room for the buns to spread slightly as well as rise. Prove for about 25 minutes, or until well risen, then bake in a an preheated oven set to 230°C (450°F), Gas Mark 8 for 12 minutes. Allow to cool then cover with a thin layer of icing made by mixing sifted icing sugar with a little water. Eat the buns while they are fresh.
Make the Swiss Buns more interesting by kneading grated lemon or orange zest into the dough and mixing the icing sugar with the fruit juice or sifting some cocoa powder with the icing sugar.

☆ ☆ ☆ ☆ ☆ ☆ ☆ ☆ ☆ ☆ ☆ ☆ ☆ ☆ ☆ ☆ ☆ ☆ ☆ ☆ ☆ ☆ ☆ ☆

☆ ☆ ☆ ☆ ☆ ☆ ☆ ☆ ☆ ☆ ☆ ☆ ☆ ☆ ☆ ☆ ☆ ☆ ☆ ☆ ☆ ☆ ☆ ☆ ☆ ☆ ☆

# RING DOUGHNUTS

No-one had sufficient fat to cook proper round doughnuts. These
doughnuts, based on the Home-made Bread (see page 28) are
fairly flat, so they can be fried in the minimum of cooking fat.
To make ring doughnuts, allow the bread dough to prove, then
take off the amount required. Roll out on a lightly floured
board and cut into rings with two different-sized cutters.
Place on a baking tray and allow to prove for about
25 minutes, or until well risen.
Heat 1–2 oz (25–50g) fat in a frying pan and put in the
doughnuts. Fry quickly on either side until golden in colour then
reduce the heat and cook steadily for about 5 minutes. Lift
out and drain on crumpled tissue paper, if you have it
(use kitchen paper today), then roll in a little sugar.

☆ ☆ ☆ ☆ ☆ ☆ ☆ ☆ ☆ ☆ ☆ ☆ ☆ ☆ ☆ ☆ ☆ ☆ ☆ ☆ ☆ ☆ ☆ ☆ ☆ ☆ ☆

## MALT AND FRUIT BREAD

*Preparation time: 15 minutes*
*Cooking time: 1 hour*
*Quantity: 1 loaf*

In 1946, many parents gave their
children extract of malt for health
reasons; it also made an excellent
flavouring for a baking powder bread.
The recipe can be varied by using
powdered malt or Ovaltine (see
Variation, right).

2 level tablespoons malt extract
2 level tablespoons golden syrup
2–4 oz (50–115 g) dried
  fruit
5 tablespoons milk or
  milk and water
8 oz (225 g) self
  raising flour or plain
  flour with 2 teaspoons
  baking powder
½ level teaspoon
  bicarbonate of soda
pinch salt
1 egg

Grease and flour a 1½ lb (675 g)
loaf tin. Preheat the oven to 180°C
(350°F), Gas Mark 4. Put the malt,
syrup and milk, or milk and water,
into a saucepan and heat gently until
melted. Add the fruit to the hot
mixture and leave until cold.

Sift the flour, or flour and baking
powder, with the bicarbonate of soda

and salt. Add the malt mixture then
the egg. Beat well and spoon into the
prepared tin. Bake for 50–60 minutes
or until firm to the touch. Cool in the
tin for 5 minutes then turn out.

### VARIATION

Use powdered malt or Ovaltine and
mix this with the flour. Melt the syrup
with ¼ pint (150 ml) milk as in the
recipe above, then add the fruit.
Allow to cool then continue as the
recipe.

## HALFPAY PUDDING

This pudding is a traditional English
recipe, adapted to the lack of fat in
1946. When bread rationing began in
July it would not have been made.
The high percentage of breadcrumbs
makes it a very light pudding.

*Preparation time: 15 minutes*
*Cooking time: 1½ hours*
*Quantity: 4 helpings*

2 oz (50g) self-raising flour with
  ½ teaspoon baking powder
  or plain flour with 1 teaspoon
  baking powder
4 oz (115 g) soft breadcrumbs
pinch salt
2 oz (50 g) shredded suet
1–2 oz (25–50g) sultanas
1–2 oz (25–50g) currants
2 tablespoons golden syrup
little milk

**For the sauce:**
3 tablespoons golden syrup

Sift the flour and baking powder into
a bowl, add the rest of the ingredients,
using enough milk to make a mixture
with a sticky consistency.

Put the golden syrup for the sauce
into a greased 1½ pint (900 ml) basin
and add the pudding mixture. Cover
tightly and steam over boiling water
for 40 minutes, then lower the heat to
simmering for a further 45 minutes.
Serve hot.

### VARIATION

If suet is not avail-
able, use melted
margarine instead.

# ★1947★

THIS YEAR IS memorable because of the exceptionally long and cold winter. It started in 1946 and continued throughout the spring of 1947. Frozen pipes were a feature in many houses, for few had central heating or good protection against frost. Transport was bad due to the weather.

Bread rationing continued during this year until July but, apart from rationing, supplies of food and coal were difficult because of transport problems.

The Government was anxious to increase our exports, most of which had been lost during the war years, so women were being persuaded to work in factories and elsewhere.

Lord Woolton was honoured at the Mansion House for his work at the Ministry of Food during the war years and praised for the effectiveness of the Ministry's Food Facts which gave information and recipes to inspire cooks.

The showing of Christian Dior's New Look fashions in the spring created a great deal of excitement for women. At last we were seeing glamorous and flattering styles, so different from the Utility clothes of recent years.

The engagement of Princess Elizabeth to Prince Philip Mountbatten and their wedding celebrations later in the year were inspirng and joyous events. The splendour of the pageantry and ceremonial of the wedding day was like a breath of new life in the midst of the somewhat dreary and uninspired existence of these early post-war years. The Government announced that extra clothing coupons would be allocated for the wedding dress but that Princess Elizabeth would not have a trousseau due to the clothing restrictions.

Some gadgets for the home began to appear on the market but not as many as people wanted. Refrigerators were being made but many went for export. Icing pipes and syringes became very popular, although we really had no extra sugar for piped icing, and cream was still unavailable. Mock cream or butter icing (generally made with margarine) were used to decorate cakes. Some nuts came on the market in time for Christmas. Whale meat, which was not on ration, became more readily available and the Ministry of Food gave suggestions and recipes for using it: I have included two recipes using whale meat in this chapter.

In November, the first women's television magazine programme was started by the BBC. I was the television cook on this programme and for many years to come. My first recipe before the cameras was 8-Minute Doughnuts, the recipe for which I have included here. Philip Harben had preceded me as a television chef and from time to time both of us appeared on the same programme.

In May, there were reports that the Ministry of Food was thinking of getting supplies of horsemeat to augment the meat ration. Most people viewed this with horror and fortunately nothing came of the idea.

A little extra meat, sugar and sweets were made available for Christmas 1947. The extra rations were very welcome, for this had been a difficult year with bad weather lasting to the spring and shortages of many foods.

For some families this was the first Christmas when everyone was together. In 1946 many men and women were still serving abroad in the armed forces.

☆ ☆ ☆ ☆ ☆ ☆ ☆ ☆ ☆ ☆ ☆ ☆ ☆ ☆ ☆ ☆ ☆ ☆ ☆ ☆ ☆ ☆ ☆ ☆ ☆

# WHALE MEAT

Over the years I have been asked repeatedly to describe whale meat. Nowadays, we would be horrified at the thought of using these magnificent and protected mammals for food, but in 1946 we were anxious to have more generous helpings of meat so the Government were ready to persuade us to avail ourselves of this unrationed 'bonus', which became better known in 1947. Whale meat looked like a cross between liver and beef, with a firm texture. Because the raw meat had a strong and very unpleasant smell of fish and stale oil, I loathed handling whale meat to create recipes or to use in my demonstrations to the public. When cooked, the smell was not apparent.

The Ministry of Food's *Food and Nutrition* booklet for September 1947 included advice on preparing and cooking whale meat: 'Tests were made in our Experimental Kitchens using the best cuts of whale meat, which was bought in its frozen state, thawed out slowly and treated as ordinary beef steak. It was found that although the raw meat looked somewhat unattractive and is not very satisfactory grilled or cooked as a joint, most people cannot distinguish it from beef steak when it is finely cut before cooking or mixed with strong flavours.'

## HAMBURGERS

*Preparation time: 15 minutes*
*Cooking time: 15 or 30 minutes*
*(see method)*
*Quantity: 4 helpings*

I demonstrated this recipe at Harrods, which shows that the liking for hamburgers in Britain goes a long way back.

1 large potato, grated
1 medium onion, finely chopped
12 oz (350 g) minced whale
  meat or beef
1 teaspoon Worcestershire sauce
½–1 tablespoon chopped parsley
salt and pepper

**For the coating:**
crisp breadcrumbs (optional)

Mix all the ingredients together, form into round cakes. These can be rolled in crisp breadcrumbs, although this is not essential.

Either grill for 15 minutes or bake on a greased baking tray for 30 minutes in a preheated oven set to 190°C (375°F), Gas Mark 5.

When fat is available, the Hamburgers can be fried.

☆ ☆ ☆ ☆ ☆ ☆ ☆ ☆ ☆ ☆ ☆ ☆ ☆ ☆ ☆ ☆ ☆ ☆ ☆ ☆ ☆ ☆ ☆ ☆ ☆

## HUNGARIAN GOULASH

*Preparation time: 20 minutes*
*Cooking time: 2 hours*
*Quantity: 4 helpings*

This recipe comes from the Ministry of Food's *Food and Nutrition* booklet for September 1947, in which they gave advice on using whale meat.

    2 lb (900 g) onions, sliced *
    1½–2 oz (40–50g) dripping
        or cooking fat
    4 level teaspoons paprika
    2–3 teaspoons salt **
    ¼ level teaspoon pepper
    1 lb (450 g) whale meat, cut
        into 1 inch (2.5 cm) cubes

* The high proportion of onions is because at this time of the year British onions were plentiful.
** Ministry recipes tend to be generous with salt. No liquid is given in the ingredients but it was assumed one would cover the food with water or beef stock.

Fry the onions in the melted dripping or fat in a saucepan until pale golden brown, taking care not to let them burn. Add the seasonings and stir well. Place the meat in the pan with the other ingredients and the liquid. Cover the pan and simmer for 2 hours.

### VARIATIONS

Use stewing beef or boned neck of mutton or lamb instead of whale meat or mix two meats together in true Hungarian style, i.e. whale meat and pork, or beef and pork, or lamb and beef.

NOVEMBER-DECEMBER, 1947

KITCHEN GARDEN

JOAN MARTIN MAY

*Recipes by the Ministry of Food.*
*Gardening Instructions by the Ministry of Agriculture.*

## Apple Pudding — NEW STYLE

SAYS PATRICIA SEYMOUR:
*"This is a recipe to keep among your favourites!"*

I THINK this Apple Batter Pudding is a winner! It's best made in a "Pyrex" brand casserole. This lovely glassware cooks food evenly all through. Also, you save messy washing up of saucepans.

You need 1 lb. of apples (or other fruit) and 2½ oz. sugar. For the batter: 6 oz. self-raising flour; pinch salt; 1 level teaspn. mixed spice; ½ oz. margarine; 1½ teacups milk and water; ½ oz. sugar; ½ teaspoon lemon essence.

Sift flour, salt, and spice, rub in fat, then mix in sugar. Beat in half the liquid gradually. Beat *thoroughly*, then mix in rest of liquid and lemon essence.

Peel apples, cut in small pieces and mix with 2 oz. sugar. Put in a greased casserole and pour batter over. Bake in a moderate oven for about ¾ of an hour. Sprinkle with remaining sugar and serve *hot*.

The 12 months' free replacement guarantee of "Pyrex" brand ovenware (against breakage by oven heat) still holds good. To make sure the guarantee is valid, get the retailer to sign and complete the guarantee form when you make your purchase; otherwise replacement cannot be made. Your dealer is authorized to replace without question upon production of this signed guarantee.

FOOD FACTS

*WHAT'S LEFT IN THE LARDER?*

## THE NEW LOOK

In June 1947 Christian Dior launched his new fashions and these caused worldwide admiration. Every newspaper and magazine carried illustrations of the clothes. They were so different from the fashions of the last decade that they were christened *The New Look*.

During recent years in Britain people had to manage with restricted amounts of clothing coupons, and any new fashions they bought were strictly utilitarian. The new line was essentially feminine with small nipped-in waists, billowing skirts and soft, gentle shoulder lines. So many younger women had been in the Services, where the uniform shoulders were rigid and square, not unlike those of a man, and they rejoiced that they would look so feminine and pretty.

The materials used were colourful and well-designed; it reflected great credit on the French fashion industry that they were able to create fashions like this so soon after the war had ended.

Sadly of course, clothing coupons had to be provided to purchase the garments, but even so, it was most women's ambition to own at least one special *New Look* dress, although few could afford a Dior garment. British fashion houses and those in other countries immediately copied the line of the revolutionary French garments. In those days a high percentage of women made their own clothes, so sewing machines were kept busy.

Later the same year Dior's autumn and winter collections were launched and the warm coats and suits reflected the same feminine look as the summer clothes. Velvet made its appearance and there was great joy to see this beautiful fabric reappear.

## HERRING AND EGG PIE

*Preparation time: 20 minutes*
*Cooking time: 40 minutes*
*Quantity: 4 helpings*

Fresh herrings were in good supply during the early part of 1947 – provided the bad weather allowed transport to distribute them. There had been disputes during the autumn of 1946, with many fishermen dissatisfied with the prices offered them by the Fishing Industry Board. Herrings were dumped back in the sea, an action which shocked the public, for wasting any food was considered a crime.

 4 large fresh herrings
 2–3 fresh tomatoes, sliced, or
  bottled tomatoes
 2 tablespoons chopped parsley
 2 tablespoons grated onion or
  finely chopped leek
 2 eggs, hard-boiled (see Chicken
  Roll, page 39, for advice on
  hard-boiling reconstituted
  dried egg)
 salt and pepper

**For the topping:**
 1 lb (450 g) cooked potatoes
 1 oz (25 g) margarine
 2 tablespoons milk
 2 oz (50 g) cheese, grated

Cut the flesh from the herrings into 1 inch (2.5 cm) dice. The roes should be finely chopped. Put in a pie dish with the sliced fresh tomatoes or well-drained bottled tomatoes, the parsley, and onion or leek; slice the eggs and add them, with a little seasoning.

For the topping, mash the potatoes with the margarine, milk, half the cheese and seasoning to taste. Spoon over the herring mixture. Top with the last of the cheese.

Bake in a preheated oven set to 190°C (375°F), Gas Mark 5 for 30 minutes. Serve hot.

*How to bone a herring before cooking*

**1.** Cut off head and remove the guts, retaining the roe. Then cut along the belly with a sharp knife or scissors.

**2.** Open fish gently, carefully loosening the small bones on each side of the backbone.

**3.** Starting at the head end, prise up backbone with thumb and forefinger and pull steadily away from the flesh.

## DUTCH MEAT PUDDING

*Preparation time: 15 minutes*
*Cooking time: 1 hour*
*Quantity: 4 helpings*

This was a way of using left-over cooked potatoes. The wartime spirit of 'waste not' still applied long after rationing ended.

 4 oz (115 g) soft breadcrumbs
 3 tablespoons milk
 1 large onion, finely chopped
  or grated
 2 large tomatoes, skinned
  and chopped
 8 oz (225 g) cooked potatoes,
  mashed
 8 oz (225 g) minced raw beef
 1 egg
 2 tablespoons finely chopped
  parsley
 2 teaspoons Worcestershire
  sauce
 salt and pepper

Put the breadcrumbs into a basin with the milk, leave soaking for 15 minutes then mix in all the other ingredients. Spoon into a 2 pint (1.2 litre) greased basin. Cover tightly and steam for 1 hour. Turn out and serve with sliced cooked beetroot.

### VARIATION

This is a good way to use up cooked meat. Follow the recipe above but steam for only 40 minutes and add rather more onion, if possible.

☆ ☆ ☆ ☆ ☆ ☆ ☆ ☆ ☆ ☆ ☆ ☆ ☆ ☆ ☆ ☆ ☆ ☆ ☆ ☆ ☆ ☆ ☆ ☆ ☆ ☆ ☆ ☆ ☆ ☆ ☆ ☆

## 8-MINUTE DOUGHNUTS

The reason I chose this recipe for my very first appearance on television was because I was told that only a boiling ring would be available. This meant I had to cook something in a frying pan or saucepan. I had found this particular recipe popular in demonstrations so repeated it before the cameras. The 'doughnuts' were fairly flat, rather like a fritter, for there was insufficient fat to fry a thicker mixture. They have a pleasant taste and were very popular with children. When these were made originally I used more baking powder than in the recipe on the right, even with self-raising flour, for the flour of 1947 was still very heavy. During recent years paper for draining fried foods had been unobtainable; now it was beginning to appear.

☆ ☆ ☆ ☆ ☆ ☆ ☆ ☆ ☆ ☆ ☆ ☆ ☆ ☆ ☆ ☆ ☆ ☆ ☆ ☆ ☆ ☆ ☆ ☆ ☆ ☆ ☆ ☆ ☆ ☆ ☆ ☆

## 8-MINUTE DOUGHNUTS

*Preparation time: 4 minutes*
*Cooking time: 8 minutes*
*Quantity: 8 cakes*

8 oz (225 g) self-raising flour or
  plain flour with 2 teaspoons
  baking powder
2 tablespoons sugar
pinch salt
2 eggs
1/4 pint (150 ml) milk

**For frying:**
2 oz (50 g) cooking fat

**For the coating:**
little sugar

Mix all the ingredients together to
form a thick batter. Heat the fat and
fry spoonfuls of the mixture for
8 minutes. Cook fairly quickly until
golden brown on all sides then lower
the heat to cook the mixture through
to the centre.

Remove from the pan, drain on
crumpled tissue paper (use kitchen
paper today) then roll in sugar.

### VARIATIONS

Add 2 tablespoons sultanas to the
mixture.

**Apple Doughnuts:** Add 1 peeled and
grated cooking apple to the mixture
and use 2 tablespoons less milk.

## SUMMER MEAT MOULD

*Preparation time: 20 minutes*
*Cooking time: 2 minutes*
*Quantity: 4–6 helpings*

After the terrible winter, the summer
of 1947 seemed particularly good
and cold dishes were required. This
was a favourite recipe. A mixture of
left-over cooked meats, beef plus
ham or chicken and ham were
favourites. Hand-operated mincing
machines were a favourite kitchen
appliance. Leaf gelatine had been
used in homes, as well as in catering
establishments, before the war but
powdered gelatine, used in this
recipe, had begun to appear.

1/2 pint (300 ml) tomato juice
2 teaspoons gelatine
12 oz (350 g) cooked meat,
  minced

## CHICKEN ROLL

*Preparation time: 30 minutes*
*Cooking time: 2 hours*
*Quantity: 8 helpings*

This is a splendid dish if enter-
taining a large number of people.
If fresh eggs are available they
should be used, though people
did hard-boil reconstituted dried
eggs. They were carefully mixed
(1 level tablespoon dried egg
powder to 2 tablespoons water),
spooned into sturdy egg cups,
covered and steamed until firm.
Although these did not look like
'proper' hard-boiled eggs they
tasted quite good for yolks and
whites were combined in the egg
powder.

1 small chicken
4 oz (115 g) soft breadcrumbs
2 tablespoons chopped
  parsley
2 tablespoons chopped
  chives or spring onions
1 teaspoon chopped thyme
  or 1/2 teaspoon dried thyme
2 eggs
4 tablespoons chicken stock
  (see method)
4 tablespoons evaporated
  milk or top of the milk

**For the filling:**
3 eggs, hard-boiled

**For the coating:**
crisp breadcrumbs (or see
  variation, right)

Cut all the flesh from the chicken
and put the bones, with oddments
of skin and giblets not required

for this recipe, into a saucepan.
Cover with water and simmer
gently for 45 minutes. Strain the
liquid. Some is used in the variation, Chaudfroid of Chicken,
below; the rest can be used in a
soup.

Mince the chicken flesh,
including the cooked or
uncooked liver from the giblets,
if liked. Blend the chicken with
all the other ingredients to make a
soft mixture. Press out to a large
oblong shape on a floured board.
Place the hard-boiled eggs in the
centre then form the chicken mixture around these to make a well-
shaped roll. Wrap the roll in well-
greased greaseproof paper or a
floured cloth.

Put the roll into a steamer
and cook for 1 1/4 hours. Carefully
remove the paper or cloth and
coat in crisp breadcrumbs. Serve
hot or cold.

### VARIATION

**Chaudfroid of Chicken:** Allow
the chicken roll to become quite
cold. Dissolve 1 level teaspoon
gelatine in 1/4 pint (150 ml) chick-
en stock. When cold, but not set,
blend with 1/4 pint (150 ml) mayonnaise or salad dressing. Leave
until fairly firm then spread over
the uncoated chicken roll with a
warmed palette knife. Garnish
with tiny pieces of radish and
tomato. Serve with various salads.

5 tablespoons finely chopped
  spring onions
2 tablespoons grated cucumber
1 tablespoon chopped parsley
1 tablespoon chopped chives
1 teaspoon chopped fresh thyme
  or 1/2 teaspoon dried thyme
salt and pepper
few drops Worcestershire sauce

Pour 3 tablespoons of the tomato
juice into a basin, sprinkle the gela-

tine on top and allow to stand for
3 minutes, then place over a pan of
hot water until dissolved. Heat the
rest of the tomato juice, add the dissolved gelatine, then stir the meat into
the hot mixture – this softens and
moistens it. Leave until cold then add
the remaining ingredients.

Spoon into a mould and allow to
set. Turn out and serve with a potato
salad and a mixed salad.

☆ ☆ ☆ ☆ ☆ ☆ ☆ ☆ ☆ ☆ ☆ ☆ ☆ ☆ ☆ ☆ ☆ ☆ ☆ ☆ ☆ ☆ ☆ ☆

## WAYS TO SERVE DRIED BANANAS

**Bananas in Salads:** Slice and soak the dried bananas in a little vinegar or water to soften slightly (although some people may prefer their firm chewy texture). Add to a green salad. Dried bananas are an excellent addition to a fresh fruit salad.

**Banana Fritters:** Halve the dried bananas, soak for a short time in water then drain well. Make up 1 quantity of 8-Minute Doughnut batter (see page 39), but add 2 tablespoons of milk, or the banana soaking liquid. Coat the bananas in the batter and fry in 2 oz (50 g) cooking fat. Heat the fat and fry the fritters for 8 minutes. cook fairly quickly until golden brown on all sides, then lower the heat to cook through to the centres. Remove from the pan and drain on crumpled tissue paper (use kitchen paper today).

☆ ☆ ☆ ☆ ☆ ☆ ☆ ☆ ☆ ☆ ☆ ☆ ☆ ☆ ☆ ☆ ☆ ☆ ☆ ☆ ☆ ☆ ☆ ☆

### FOOD FACTS

# *filling* THE PLATE

**T**HE CHILDREN at home, expectant appetites and the unexpected guest are all part of the housewife's "holiday" programme. Here are some handy fill-the-plate recipes which will help you. Cut them out and keep them by you.

**APPLE CHARLIE**

Ingredients: 6 oz. breadcrumbs, 1½ lb. apples, 1½ level tablespoons jam.

*(For 4)* Method: Grease a 1½ pint basin and press heaped spoonfuls of the breadcrumbs round the sides and on the bottom to form a lining. Peel, core and slice the apples, place in a pan with no liquid and cook gently until pulped. Beat in the jam, turn the mixture into the lined basin and cover with a layer of crumbs. Cover with a piece of greased paper and steam for ½ an hour. Turn out like a steamed pudding.

**MEAT HASH**

Ingredients: 6 oz. macaroni or 6 oz. pearl barley, 1 oz. dripping or cooking fat, 3 *(For 4)* level tablespoons flour, ½ pint vegetable stock or water, gravy browning, salt and pepper to taste. 6 oz. cooked meat, chopped, 1 lb. mixed vegetables, diced and cooked.

Method: Cook the macaroni or barley in boiling salted water. Make a brown sauce, with the fat, flour and stock or water, add a few drops of gravy browning and season well. Add the meat and vegetables and heat through. When macaroni or barley is tender, drain well, replace on a hot dish. Pile hash in centre and serve very hot.

**BAKED CARROT and ONION PIE**

Ingredients: 1½ lb. carrots, 6 oz. turnip, 8 oz. onion or leek, 4½ level tablespoons flour, ¾ *(For 4)* pint milk and vegetable stock, 1 level teaspoon salt, pinch of pepper, pinch of nutmeg, 2 oz. grated cheese, 2 slices bread (cut 1 inch thick from a large loaf) diced, 2 tablespoons melted margarine or dripping.

Method: Prepare and slice carrots, turnip, onion or leek. Boil in a little salted water until tender. Strain vegetables, keeping the liquid for the sauce, and place in a greased pie-dish. Blend the flour with a little of the cold milk, bring the rest of the liquid to the boil and pour on to the blended flour. Return to saucepan, stir until it boils and boil gently for 5 minutes. Add the seasonings and cheese and pour the sauce over the vegetables in the pie-dish; cover with the diced bread and sprinkle over the melted margarine or dripping. Bake in a hot oven for 15-20 minutes until brown on top:

*Fish Fact:* Fish landings vary—with sea weather: that is why your fishmonger sometimes has plenty, sometimes only a little. But over the whole year fish landings have been 20% more than before the war. Fish is a fine protein food. Some fish, like herrings, are rich in fat as well. Where there's fish there's a good meal.

THE MINISTRY OF FOOD, LONDON, S.W.1.     FOOD FACTS No. 390

## ORANGE AND LEMON SPONGE

*Preparation time: 25 minutes*
*Cooking time: 20 minutes*
*Quantity: 1 cake*

There were now some oranges and lemons available and they would give flavour to this cake, which would be made for a special occasion. Nothing would be wasted at this time. Citrus fruit rind was used a great deal to make marmalade, with apples providing the pulp, and to flavour cakes like this one. Reconstituted dried eggs would still be used by most people. It would have been necessary to explain to people who had not used citrus fruit in cooking for years that 'zest' was the top part of the rind, without bitter pith.

> 4 oz (115 g) margarine
> 4 oz (115 g) caster sugar
> 1 teaspoon finely grated
>   lemon zest
> 1 teaspoon finely grated
>   orange zest
> 3 eggs
> 6 oz (175 g) self-raising flour or
>   plain flour with 1½ teaspoons
>   baking powder
> ½ tablespoon lemon juice
> 1½ tablespoons orange juice

> **For the filling and decoration:**
> 4 oz (115 g) margarine
> 8 oz (225 g) icing sugar, sifted
> 1 tablespoon orange juice
> squeeze lemon juice

Preheat the oven to 180°C (350°F), Gas Mark 4. Grease and flour two 7–8 inch (18–20 cm) sandwich tins.

Cream the margarine and sugar with the fruit zest until soft and light.

Beat the eggs well and add gradually to the creamed mixture. If the mixture shows signs of curdling, then fold in some of the flour. Sift the flour, or flour and baking powder, and fold into the creamed mixture with the fruit juice. Divide the mixture between the tins and bake in the oven until firm to the touch. Turn out on to a wire cooling tray.

For the filling and decoration, cream the margarine and icing sugar together and gradually beat in the fruit juice. Use a little of the mixture to sandwich the cakes together and the remainder to spread or pipe over the top of the cake.

## BANANA AND RHUBARB COMPOTE

*Preparation time: 10 minutes*
*Cooking time: 15–20 minutes*
*Quantity: 4–6 helpings*

Dried bananas became quite popular, as they were very sweet and could be eaten without cooking; children really liked them. They had a somewhat sticky consistency. In this recipe, they help to sweeten rhubarb. The rhubarb would be the garden variety, not forced rhubarb. If using the latter, reduce the amount of water slightly.

4 dried bananas, thickly sliced
7½ fl oz (225 ml) water
1–2 tablespoons honey,
   golden syrup or sugar
1 lb (450 g) rhubarb (trimmed
   weight), neatly diced

Soak the bananas in the water for 30 minutes then simmer for 5 minutes. Add the sweetening, stir until dissolved then add the rhubarb. Cover the pan and simmer gently until just tender.

## APPLE CROQUETTES

*Preparation time: 15 minutes*
*Cooking time: 10 minutes*
*Quantity 4 helpings*

It is advisable to use the flesh from baked apples for these croquettes, since no extra water is added to the fruit. If you do stew the apples in a little water, then drain away any extra liquid.

2 large baked apples
2 tablespoons fine soft
   breadcrumbs
1 tablespoon milk or cream
pinch mixed spice
2 oz (50 g) sugar

### For the coating:
1 tablespoon flour
1 reconstituted dried egg
   (see page 10) or fresh egg
1½–2 oz (40–50 g) crisp
   breadcrumbs

### For frying:
2 oz (50 g) butter or margarine

Remove the skins of the apples and mash the pulp in a bowl. Add the rest of the ingredients. Chill until cold. Form into 8 croquette shapes. Coat in the flour, then dip in the beaten egg and roll in the crisp breadcrumbs.

Melt the butter or margarine in a frying pan and fry the croquettes until golden brown, turning them several times during the cooking process. Serve the apple croquettes with cream or the top of the milk.

### VARIATIONS

**Apple and Lemon Croquettes:** Omit the mixed spice and milk or cream. Add the finely grated zest of a lemon and 1 tablespoon of lemon juice. Serve with a little hot lemon curd.

Orange zest and juice can be used instead of lemon. Serve with hot orange marmalade.

# ★1948★

By THIS YEAR the British public were feeling more and more frustrated about the lack of food and household goods. There were many reports and rumours of people 'black-marketing', i.e. obtaining far more food than their legal rations. The Government exhorted everyone to accept the situation and not grumble.

One group of foods, preserves, was taken off the ration this year. The usual ration had been 1 lb (450 g) per person per 2 months, so it was a pleasure to know that now one could spread marmalade thickly on the breakfast toast. Preserves were also used to eke out the sugar in cooking, as you will notice in several recipes in this chapter.

The RAF were joining with American forces to drop food and fuel over Berlin to beat the Russian blockade of the city.

In the summer of 1948 there was a serious dock strike at Southampton, one of our major ports. Over 200 ships were held up, many of them carrying food from abroad. The fresh meat ration was cut to 6d (just over 2 p) and troops had to be brought in to try to save food supplies.

The 14th Olympic Games, the first to be held since 1936, were held in Britain, at the Wembley Stadium, in London. They were accounted a great success, although often christened the Austerity Olympics because of the stringent rationing and lack of special projects in this country. Germany, Japan and the Soviet Union did not participate.

Cooks sought to present food in a more elaborate and attractive manner, and wanted to entertain their friends. Cocktail parties became the vogue, for they were more practical than trying to eke out the rations to prepare dinner parties. I have included some of the cocktail party savouries of the time in this chapter.

A new fish, that received a great deal of publicity, was canned snoek. This came from South Africa, and the Ministry of Food was very anxious to promote it as a replacement for canned salmon. In spite of all the official praise, the British people hated snoek and within a relatively short time it disappeared from the shops.

The quality of fresh eggs was very poor, with eggs being stale and often bad. The Ministry now decreed that any eggs bought on ration that were bad must be replaced.

Once again, the Ministry of Food published a specially economical Christmas Cake with Mock Marzipan, and you will find recipes for both at the end of this chapter. Although more nuts were coming into Britain, including ground almonds, they were still relatively scarce and expensive.

Because we had been without nuts of any kind during the war years these were regarded as a special treat by the general public and a very necessary food by vegetarians.

We had been used to buying inexpensive monkey nuts (peanuts in their shells) before the war but now shelled peanuts were more generally available. These were also known as ground nuts.

In November 1948 the nation had a reason to rejoice. A son, Charles, was born to Princess Elizabeth and Prince Philip. The picture on page 51 shows the happy new parents at the christening of their young baby.

✩ ✩ ✩ ✩ ✩ ✩ ✩ ✩ ✩ ✩ ✩ ✩ ✩ ✩ ✩ ✩ ✩ ✩ ✩ ✩ ✩ ✩ ✩ ✩ ✩ ✩ ✩ ✩ ✩

## COCKTAIL SNACKS

These are some of the cocktail savouries that could be made in 1948. Although many basic foods were still scarce, cocktail 'nibbles' like olives and anchovy fillets were becoming available.

### Cheese Whirls

Make the biscuit dough as for Cheese Butterflies (right). Roll out to a ¼ inch (6 mm) thick oblong. Spread with Marmite. Roll firmly, like a Swiss roll, then cut into slices. Place on baking trays and brush with milk. Bake as for Cheese Butterflies.

✩ ✩ ✩ ✩ ✩ ✩ ✩ ✩ ✩ ✩ ✩ ✩ ✩ ✩ ✩ ✩ ✩ ✩ ✩ ✩ ✩ ✩ ✩ ✩ ✩ ✩ ✩ ✩ ✩

**Curried New Potatoes:** Use bite-sized potatoes. Scrub well and cook in their skins.

For 24 potatoes use 1 small onion, which should be very finely chopped or grated. Fry the onion in 1–2 oz (25–50 g) hot margarine. Add 1 teaspoon curry powder, a few drops of Worcestershire sauce and 2 tablespoons water. Add the well-drained cooked potatoes and turn around in the hot curry mixture until coated. Serve on cocktail sticks.

**Cheese Potatoes:** Cook new potatoes. When cold, cut into halves. If possible, take your cheese ration in cream cheese. Blend this with finely chopped chives and a few chopped nuts. Spread over the cut side of the potatoes.

**Princess Mushrooms:** Cook very small mushrooms then remove and set aside their stalks. Fill the mushroom caps with cream cheese or grated cheese mixed with a little margarine or mayonnaise. Garnish with the cooked stalks.

**Seafood Bites:** Top rounds of toast with peeled prawns, cooked mussels or tiny pieces of crabmeat. Garnish with a little mayonnaise and watercress leaves.

**Stuffed Eggs:** There were occasions when one could buy gulls' eggs and these were small enough to make good cocktail snacks. Cook the eggs for about 5 minutes until hardboiled. Carefully shell and halve. Remove the yolks and blend with a little anchovy essence, mashed sardines or chopped prawns. Return the filling to the white cases and place on small rounds of toast, spread with fish paste.

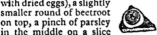

## CHEESE BUTTERFLIES

*Preparation time: 15 minutes*
*Cooking time: 12–15 minutes*
*Quantity: 15 canapés*

Use these economical cheese biscuits within a day or so of baking. Store in an airtight tin before filling with the cream cheese. The biscuits are a good way to use up the ends of cheese that may have gone hard and can be grated very finely.

6 oz (175 g) plain flour
salt and pepper
1/2 teaspoon mustard powder
2 oz (50 g) cooking fat
  or margarine
2 oz (50 g) Cheddar
  cheese, grated
1 egg

**For the filling:**
1 oz (25 g) margarine
1 level tablespoon dried
  milk powder
2 tablespoons finely
  grated cheese
pinch mustard powder
few drops vinegar
little milk

Preheat the oven to 180°C (350°F), Gas Mark 4. Grease flat baking trays.

Sift the flour with the seasonings, rub in the fat or margarine and add the cheese. Mix well then gradually add enough beaten egg to make a dough with a firm rolling consistency.

Roll out thinly and cut into approximately 30 small rounds. Cut half the rounds down the centre to form the wings. Place on greased, flat baking trays and bake until pale golden in colour and firm to the touch. Allow to cool on the trays.

Cream the margarine with the milk powder, cheese, mustard and vinegar. Gradually add a little milk to give a firm spreading consistency. Spread or pipe a line of filling on the biscuit rounds then place the 'wings' in position.

### A MODERN TOUCH

Increase the amount of fat and cheese in the biscuits to 3 oz (85 g). Omit the milk powder in the filling and double the amount of cheese.

**DO YOU KNOW** what traffic is?

TRAFFIC is everyone on the roads, streets, and pavements. Whether walking, riding or driving, we are all part of it. Any one of us can cause an accident — or help to prevent one.

If everything went at one mile an hour, there might be no accidents. But, for all our sakes, traffic must *move* — as swiftly as is safe. Road Navigation (based on the Highway Code) is the art of getting about easily, swiftly and *safely* — and helping others to do the same. It's largely a matter of considering others *on* the road, as most of us do *off* the road. It will pay us all to become skilful Road Navigators.

**GET HOME SAFE AND SOUND**

*Issued by the Ministry of Transport*

## AVOCADO CANAPÉS

*Preparation time: 5 minutes*
*No cooking*
*Quantity: 12–16 canapés*

Avocados began to appear in large towns and good greengrocers. They were called avocado pears at first, which gave people the idea that they were just like an ordinary pear. When first sampled, they were disliked by many people, unprepared for the new taste. As people became accustomed to the taste, avocados became more and more popular.

1 large or 2 smaller ripe
  avocados
1 tablespoon lemon juice
salt and pepper
3 teaspoons finely chopped
  or grated onion
2 teaspoons olive oil or
  melted margarine
12–16 small savoury biscuits or
  rounds of bread and butter
12–16 small peeled prawns
  or shrimps

Halve and peel the avocado(s), remove the stone(s) and mash the pulp with the lemon juice and seasoning. Add the onion with the oil or margarine and spoon on to the biscuits or bread. Top with the prawns or shrimps.

### VARIATION

The avocado mixture makes an excellent sandwich filling or a topping for grilled or baked white fish.

## SNOEK

As a Ministry leaflet explained, 'Already we have seen people pulling wry faces at the mention of snoek; many of them who have never tasted it have assured us it is too salty; others regard it as 'ersatz' (this word, meaning a poor imitation, had become much used during the war). Why has the Ministry of Food imported this fish? The answer is that its purchase is part of our policy of replacing foods previously imported from dollar sources by foods produced within the sterling area. 'The price is reasonable: 1s 4½d (7.5 p) for ½ lb (225 g). This compares with 2s 4½d (12.5 p) for ½ lb (225 g) red salmon and 1s 6d (8 p) for Group 3 (pink) salmon. The point value is, at the moment, very low: 1 point for the ½ lb (225 g) as compared with red salmon 14 points and Group 3 (pink) 6 points.'

**RECIPE of the WEEK**

## SNOEK AND TOMATO DISH

*Preparation time: 10 minutes*
*Cooking time: 6 minutes*
*Quantity: 4 helpings*

Snoek is a cousin to mackerel, sword-fish and tuna. It is found in the seas round southern Africa. In Australia, the fish is known as barracuda and in Chile as sierra.

- 1 oz (25 g) dripping or cooking fat
- 8 oz (225 g) spring onions, chopped
- 1 lb (450 g) tomatoes, skinned and sliced
- 1 x 8 oz (225 g) can snoek, flaked
- 1 teaspoon sugar
- salt and pepper

Melt the fat, put in the onions and cook until golden brown; add the tomatoes and cook gently until tender. Add the snoek, sugar and seasoning and cook gently until thoroughly hot. Serve with potatoes and a green vegetable.

**A MODERN TOUCH**
Use canned tuna or salmon for this dish.

" Steady, now, mother. If it springs at you I'll slosh it with this axe."

## COFFEE CREAMS

*Preparation time: 15 minutes*
*Cooking time: 10 minutes*
*Quantity: 4 helpings*

By 1948 it had become easier to buy better quality instant and ground coffee, so coffee-lovers enjoyed a better beverage. We tended to use coffee flavouring a great deal in desserts and cakes, for it was such a pleasure to have this.

- 1 oz (25 g) cornflour
- ¼ pint (150 ml) milk
- ½ pint (300 ml) moderately strong coffee
- 2 oz (50 g) sugar, preferably soft brown
- 7½ fl oz (250 ml) unsweetened evaporated milk, whipped (see Economical Ice Creams, page 59)

**To decorate:**
whipped evaporated milk or Mock Cream (see page 71) little grated chocolate

Blend the cornflour with the cold milk. Bring the coffee to the boil, pour over the cornflour and mix well. Return to the saucepan with the sugar and stir over a low heat until thick- ened. Cover with a damp piece of greaseproof paper to prevent a skin forming and leave until cool, then fold in the whipped evaporated milk. Spoon into glasses and leave until quite cold.

To decorate, top with more evaporated milk or Mock Cream and grated chocolate.

## MOIST ORANGE CAKE

*Preparation time: 15 minutes*
*Cooking time: 50 minutes*
*Quantity: 1 cake*

Preserves help to save sugar in baking but do measure them carefully, for too generous an amount would make the cake heavy.

6 oz (175 g) self-raising flour or plain flour with 1½ teaspoons baking powder
½ level teaspoon bicarbonate of soda
2 oz (50 g) margarine or cooking fat
4 level tablespoons orange marmalade
1 teaspoon finely grated orange zest or few drops orange essence
2 oz (50 g) sugar
6 tablespoons orange juice or milk
2 eggs

Preheat the oven to 160°C (325°F), Gas Mark 3. Line an oblong tin measuring 7 x 4 inches (18 x 10 cm) and at least 2 inches (5 cm) deep with greased greaseproof paper.

Sift the flour, or flour and baking powder, with the bicarbonate of soda into a mixing bowl. Put the margarine or cooking fat, marmalade, orange zest or essence and the sugar into a saucepan. Stir over a low heat until melted. Add to the flour. Heat the orange juice or milk in the saucepan in which the ingredients were melted, stirring well so nothing is wasted. Add to the flour and beat vigorously. Lastly, add the eggs and beat again.

Spoon the mixture into the prepared tin and bake for 50 minutes, or until the cake is firm to the touch. Leave to cool in the tin for 30 minutes then turn out.

## APRICOT AND LEMON FLAN

*Preparation time: 25 minutes*
*Cooking time: 30 minutes*
*Quantity: 4–6 helpings*

Jam tarts were made with a somewhat sparse amount of apricot jam during rationing but this recipe, with its generous amount of jam, became possible when preserves came off ration in 1948.

New cooks may not have baked pastry cases 'blind', the term for baking an empty pastry case. Simply put greased greaseproof paper (greased side downwards) into the pastry shape, top with crusts of bread (these can be used afterwards for rusks) or pieces of macaroni. This method keeps the pastry base flat during cooking.

Shortcrust pastry made with 6 oz (175 g) flour etc. (see Gypsy Tart, page 21)

**For the filling:**
1 oz (25 g) margarine
1 teaspoon finely grated lemon zest
5 tablespoons apricot jam
1 oz (25 g) fine soft breadcrumbs
1 egg
1 tablespoon lemon juice

Preheat the oven to 190°C (375°F), Gas Mark 5. Make the pastry, roll out and use to line a 7–8 inch (18–20 cm) flan dish or tin or a flan ring placed on an upturned baking tray.

Bake the pastry case blind for 10 minutes only, removing it from the oven and reducing the oven temperature to 180°C (350°F), Gas Mark 4.

Meanwhile, cream the margarine for the filling and add the rest of the ingredients. Spoon the mixture into the partially cooked pastry case, return to the oven and bake for a further 20 minutes. Serve hot or cold.

## DOCK STRIKE

As explained on page 43, there was a dock strike in the summer of 1948 and as all foodstuffs were so valuable the Forces had to be called in to help distribute these. Servicemen also came to the rescue in January of the previous year. This was due to the stoppage by road haulage workers. Although the dockers did not come out on strike they gave support to the strikers by blacking any goods that were due to be carried by road. This dispute, like the later one in 1948, affected supplies of fresh meat badly and many homes had to depend upon the old standby — corned beef — when they could not purchase fresh meat. Favourite recipes using this canned beef were brought into use, see below.

Another serious dock strike occured in October 1954, when it was estimated that 51,000 workers were affected. By this time of course supplies of food were more plentiful but it was reported that the strike cut Britain's sea trade by half.

### USE CORNED BEEF

**To make fritters:** coat sliced beef with egg and crumbs and fry until crisp.

**To grill:** slice and brush with a little melted fat; grill for a few minutes.

**To roast:** do not slice the beef, brush the outside with a little melted fat, coat in chopped herbs and roast until piping hot. Serve with roast onions and roast potatoes.

**Cheese Toasts:** mash the corned beef, flavour with a little Worcestershire sauce and a skinned chopped tomato. Place on hot toast, top with grated cheese and put under the grill until the cheese melts.

Use diced corned beef in a Shepherd's Pie: in a casserole with finely chopped vegetables: as a sandwich filling.

*What on earth can I pack for his lunch tomorrow?*

## MOCK MARZIPAN

*Preparation time: 10 minutes*
*No cooking*
*Quantity: enough to cover top of*
*7 inch (18 cm) cake*

2 oz (50 g) margarine
2 oz (50 g) caster or icing
   sugar, sifted
1–2 teaspoons almond essence
8 oz (225 g) plain cake crumbs

Cream the margarine and sugar with the essence. Add the crumbs and knead the mixture. Roll out.

## MINISTRY OF FOOD CHRISTMAS CAKE

This was the recommended recipe from the Ministry of Food both in 1947 and again in 1948. The ingredients make a very acceptable fruit cake.

*Preparation time: 20 minutes*
*Cooking time: 2½ hours*
*Quantity: 1 cake*

4 oz (115 g) margarine
3 oz (85 g) sugar, preferably
   soft brown
2 reconstituted dried eggs
   (see page 10) or fresh eggs
3 level tablespoons warmed
   golden syrup or treacle *
8 oz (225 g) plain flour
pinch salt
½ level teaspoon bicarbonate
   of soda **
1 level teaspoon ground
   cinnamon
1 level teaspoon mixed spice
1 lb (450 g) mixed dried fruit
3 tablespoons cold well-strained
   tea

* Warm the syrup or treacle then measure it.
** Do not exceed this amount.

Line a 7 inch (18 cm) cake tin with greased greaseproof paper. Preheat the oven to 150°C (300°F), Gas Mark 2.

Cream the margarine and sugar. Gradually add the beaten eggs then the syrup or treacle. Sift all the dry ingredients together then add to the creamed mixture with the fruit and tea. Spoon into the cake tin and make a hollow in the centre so the cake will stay flat on top. Bake for 2½ hours or until firm to the touch and the sides have slightly shrunk away from the tin. Cool in the tin.

When cold remove from the tin; store in an airtight container.

# ★1949★

ALTHOUGH THERE WAS to be no further permanent de-rationing of major
foodstuffs for several years, on the whole the
food situation was less grim than in the past.
Many more unrationed foods were becoming plentiful. There were reasonable supplies
of imported fruits and vegetables as well as
seasonal home-grown varieties. Chickens
and other poultry, rabbits and pigeons were
to be found in the shops and the variety of
fish was greater and the quality better.
There were some complaints that expensive
restaurants and hotels were 'snapping up'
unrationed food.

There was a temporary drop in the rations of
sugar in the summer of 1949, due to a dollar
shortage and, for the same reason, the sweet
ration was drastically reduced to 4 oz (115 g)
from the usual 12 oz (350 g) per month. Britain
had to devalue the pound by 30 per cent.

A Ministry of Food report in this year noted
that there were hopes that Australia would
build up its meat supplies, so that it would sup-
plant the Argentine as our main supplier of
imported meat.

The Ministry of Food booklets continued to
stress the importance of a nutritional diet.

A survey done in this year stressed the
growth of eating out in Britain. For many
people, the habit had begun in the war years
when they ate at British Restaurants, which had
served simple and inexpensive meals.

Clothes rationing, which was introduced in
1941, ended in July but Utility clothes, made to
fairly strict guidelines, were still to be available
in the shops and these would be cheaper than
more elaborate garments.

There was great enthusiasm for the new
Pressure Saucepans. Pressure cookers had been
made in the past but they had been large and
heavy. The modern pans were the size of a large
saucepan and very easy to use. The pans were
quite revolutionary, for they cooked food within minutes, rather than the hours needed for
dishes like stews. The flavour and nutrients of
the food were retained and, because of the short
cooking period, an appreciable amount of fuel
was saved.

Throughout the war years, when people bottled fruit, they had asked me about bottling
vegetables. This was not possible in an oven or
ordinary sterilizer, for the temperature was not
sufficiently high to destroy harmful bacteria
that could cause botulism. A pressure cooker,
which reached higher temperatures, made vegetable bottling practical and safe.

The demand for refrigerators had been
steadily growing, for people had realized their
advantages in storing food at safe temperatures,
as well as allowing one to make delectable cold
dishes, including ices and sorbets. Before the
war, it was recorded that only 250,000 homes
in Britain had a refrigerator; gradually throughout the 1950s that number rose until by 1961
twenty-three per cent of all homes had one.

Britain had to wait for home freezers to
come on the market. The small freezing
compartment in the refrigerators of this era
were only sufficiently deep to contain freezing
trays for making ice or shallow containers so
people used these for freezing ice cream or
sorbets. The temperature in the freezing
compartment was too high to contemplate
freezing other foods.

# PRESSURE COOKERS

The new small pressure cookers (known as pressure pans) caused a sensation. The idea of being able to cook a stew within minutes, rather than hours, was much appreciated. There were still severe fuel cuts and we were urged to save fuel which, of course, was possible with the shorter pressure cooking times. Some people found the initial sound of the pans as they came to pressure a little alarming, so I had to reassure both the press and the public that they were safe and that the results of cooking all kinds of food were very satisfactory.

I wrote the first pressure cooking book for Harrods. The recipes from it I have included here typify the foods we cooked at that time.

**Pressure cooking tip**
When using a recipe that is made with self-raising flour, or uses baking powder, the mixture must be steamed, without pressure, for the first part of the cooking period so that the mixture rises.

**Adapting pressure cooker times:**
If you do not possess a pressure cooker the recipes that follow can be cooked by the usual means; here are timings:

**Dried Pea Soup:** 1¾–2 hours cooking. Use double the amount of water.
**Cod and Tomato Savoury:** 25 minutes in a steamer.
**Beef Stew:** 2–2½ hours simmering. Use double the amount of water.
**Steak and Kidney Pudding:** 3 hours steaming.
**Brigade Pudding:** 2 hours steaming.
**Brown Betty Pudding:** 1¾ hours steaming.

## DRIED PEA SOUP

*Preparation time: overnight soaking*
*Cooking time: 20 minutes*
*pressure cooking*
*Quantity: 4–6 helpings*

Dried peas had been available throughout the years of rationing and were an item on the points system. The problem about them was that they needed prolonged cooking after soaking. The pressure cooker meant they could be cooked in a relatively short time.

The very new liquidizers (blenders) that became available meant you could use one instead of rubbing ingredients through a sieve in the traditional manner – another excellent time saver.

8 oz (225 g) dried peas
2 onions
2 carrots
1 small turnip, optional
1 pint (600 ml) water
1 teaspoon sugar
1 sprig mint or pinch dried mint
salt and pepper

Cover the peas with cold water and soak overnight.

Peel and chop the onion, carrot and turnip neatly if you do not want to sieve or liquidize the soup. If you intend to serve it as a smooth soup, then chop the vegetables quite coarsely.

Drain the peas and put into the pressure cooker, do not use the trivet (rack). Add the other ingredients. Fix the lid and bring up to pressure. Maintain for 20 minutes. Allow the pressure to drop to room temperature.

Sieve or liquidize the ingredients then return to the pressure cooker, without the lid, to heat.

### VARIATIONS

Add a little top of the milk before serving the soup.

**Butter Bean Soup:** Use butter beans instead of dried peas with the same vegetables plus 1 or 2 tomatoes, if available. Substitute a sprig of parsley for the mint and allow 30 minutes pressure cooking time.

Both the Dried Pea Soup and the Butter Bean Soup can be soaked, drained and then cooked in an ordinary saucepan for 1¼–2 hours. Use 2 pints (1.2 litres) of water for cooking and cover the pan tightly.

## BEEF STEW

*Preparation time: 15 minutes*
*Cooking time: 5 minutes, then*
*15 minutes pressure cooking*
*Quantity: 4 helpings*

1 lb (450 g) stewing steak
salt and pepper
2 medium onions
4 medium carrots
1 medium turnip
1 oz (25 g) dripping or fat
¾ pint (450 ml) water
little gravy flavouring or
   yeast extract
1 oz (25 g) flour
1 tablespoon chopped parsley

Cut the steak into neat 1 inch (2.5 cm) cubes and season lightly. Peel and dice the vegetables. Heat the dripping or fat in the bottom of the pressure cooker then add the steak and cook quickly for 5 minutes. Turn the meat during this time so it browns on all sides.

Add ½ pint (300 ml) of the water with any flavouring required plus the vegetables. Fix the lid and bring to pressure. Maintain this for 15 minutes. Cool rapidly under cold water then remove the lid. Blend the flour with the rest of the water, add to the pan and stir over a moderate heat until the liquid thickens. Taste, adjust the seasoning and add the parsley.

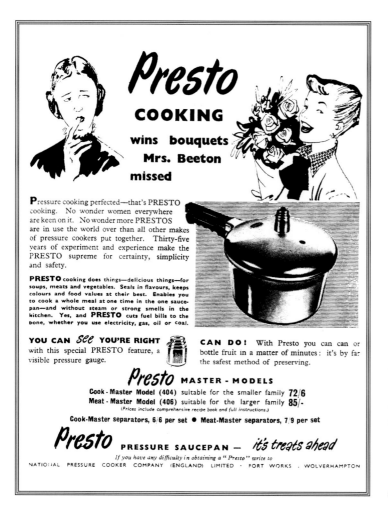
## COD AND TOMATO SAVOURY

This dish was a good one to demonstrate that ovenproof glassware was safe in the high heat of a pressure cooker.

*Preparation time: 5 minutes*
*Cooking time: 4 minutes pressure cooking*
*Quantity: 4 helpings*

1 onion, grated
8 oz (225 g) tomatoes, sliced
2 tablespoons chopped parsley
2 tablespoons breadcrumbs
salt and pepper
12 oz (350 g) cod or other white fish, without bones or skin

Grease an ovenproof dish that will fit inside the pressure cooker.

Mix the onion, tomatoes, parsley and breadcrumbs. Season the mixture. Spoon half into the bottom of the dish, add the fish, then add the rest of the tomato mixture.

Put the trivet into the pressure-cooker, add ½ pint (300 ml) water. Stand the dish on the trivet. Fix the lid and bring to pressure. Maintain this for 4 minutes then allow it to drop to room temperature.

## STEAK AND KIDNEY PUDDING

*Preparation time: 30 minutes*
*Cooking time: 30 minutes steaming plus 55 minutes pressure cooking*
*Quantity: 4–6 helpings*

**For the suet crust pastry:**
8 oz (225 g) flour etc.
  (see Brigade Pudding, page 57)

**For the filling:**
1 lb (450 g) stewing steak
4–6 oz (115–175 g) ox or lambs' kidneys, skinned
1 tablespoon flour
salt and pepper
little stock or water

Prepare the suet crust pastry and line the basin (see Brigade Pudding, page 57). Dice the meats for the filling.

Blend the flour with the seasoning, roll the meat in this mixture then put into the pastry-lined basin. Add enough stock or water to come half-way up the meat. Roll out the remaining pastry for the lid, place in position then cover the pudding.

Pour 2 pints (1.2 litres) boiling water into the pressure cooker. Stand the pudding on the trivet. Fix the lid and steam the pudding for 30 minutes. Bring up to pressure and cook for 55 minutes. Allow the pressure to drop to room temperature then serve.

**VARIATIONS:**
Steam the pudding for about 3 hours.
**Rabbit or Chicken Pudding:** Use diced rabbit or chicken and sliced onions instead of the meat. If the rabbit or chicken is young the pressure cooking time can be reduced to 35 minutes. For older flesh follow the cooking time above.

**A MODERN TOUCH**
Use the weight that gives LOW pressure and allow 1 hour pressure cooking time. If cooking young rabbit or chicken, allow 40 minutes.

## BROWN BETTY PUDDING

*Preparation time: 20 minutes*
*Cooking time: 30 minutes*
*pressure cooking*
*Quantity: 4–6 helpings*

This pudding is excellent when prepared in a pressure cooker.

1½ oz (40 g) margarine
4 oz (115 g) soft brown
    breadcrumbs
1 lb (450 g) cooking apples,
    weight when peeled and cored
2 oz (50 g) sugar
2 oz (50 g) sultanas or other
    dried fruit
½–1 teaspoon mixed spice
2 level tablespoons golden syrup
1 tablespoon water

Use just under half the margarine to grease a 1½–2 pint (900 ml–1.2 litre) basin then coat with a scant 1 oz (25 g) of the crumbs. Peel, core and slice the apples, mix with the sugar, dried fruit and spice.

Fill the basin with alternate layers of crumbs and apple mixture, beginning and ending with crumbs. Mix the syrup with the water, pour over the pudding then top with the rest of the margarine, cut in small pieces.

Cover the pudding with a plate or greaseproof paper. Fill the cooker with 2 pints (1.2 litres) boiling water. Stand the pudding on the trivet. Fix the lid and bring up to pressure. Maintain this for 30 minutes. Allow the pressure to drop to room temperature. Serve the pudding with custard.

## BRIGADE PUDDING

*Preparation time: 30 minutes*
*Cooking time: 30 minutes steaming plus 25 minutes pressure cooking*
*Quantity: 4–6 helpings*

One of the advantages for cooks at this time was that more suet could now be obtained, either from the butcher or as shredded suet in packets. Suet was a favourite form of fat for sweet and savoury puddings. It had been extremely difficult to obtain in the wartime years.

**For the suet crust pastry:**
8 oz (225 g) self-raising
    flour or plain flour with 2
    teaspoons baking powder
½ teaspoon salt, or to taste
2–4 oz (50–115 g) shredded
    suet
water, to bind

**For the filling:**
1 lb (450 g) cooking apples
2 oz (50 g) soft breadcrumbs
2 oz (50 g) currants
1 tablespoon marmalade
3 tablespoons golden syrup

For the pastry, sift the flour, or flour and baking powder, with the salt. Add the suet and enough water to make a soft rolling consistency. Roll the pastry out thinly and use about three-quarters to line a lightly greased 1½–2 pint (900 ml–1.2 litre) basin.

For the filling, peel, core and thinly slice the apples, mix with the other ingredients and spoon into the pastry-lined basin. Roll out the remaining pastry to form a lid. Seal the edges firmly and cover. Pour 2 pints (1.2 litres) boiling water into the pressure cooker. Stand the basin on the trivet. Fix the lid but DO NOT add the weight. Steam steadily for 30 minutes. Bring to pressure and cook for 25 minutes. Allow the pressure to drop to room temperature then serve the pudding hot with custard.

### VARIATIONS
Steam the pudding for 2 hours over steadily boiling water.

**Apple Pudding:** Use 1½ lb (675 g) sliced apples with a little sugar and 2 tablespoons water as the filling.

Other fruits can be used as a filling, i.e. rhubarb and soft fruits. Instead of using suet rub 2–4 oz (50–115 g) margarine or cooking fat into the flour.

### A MODERN TOUCH
Use the weight that gives LOW pressure and allow 30 minutes cooking time.

## IRISH SODA BREAD

*Preparation time: 10 minutes*
*Cooking time: 30 minutes*
*Quantity: 1 loaf*

Although bread rationing had long been over, many people were still keen on baking bread. They had tried to make good soda bread during 1946 and 1947, when bread was rationed, and had been very disappointed. The flour of those days was very heavy. By 1949 flour was improving and it was possible to get a good result.

The variation using potatoes (right) gives another excellent and light bread.

1 lb (450 g) plain flour
½ teaspoon salt
½ level teaspoon bicarbonate
    of soda
1 level teaspoon cream of tartar
½ pint (300 ml) milk or
    milk and water

Preheat the oven to 220°C (425°F), Gas Mark 7. Sift the dry ingredients and bind to a soft but not over-sticky dough with the liquid. Form into a large round about 1 inch (2.5 cm) thick. Put on to a baking tray. Mark into sections (known as farls). Bake for 30 minutes.

NOTE: if you can obtain buttermilk, use only ½ teaspoon cream of tartar.

### VARIATIONS
**Potato Soda Bread:** Use only 8 oz (225 g) flour with the same amounts of salt, bicarbonate of soda and cream of tartar. Add 8 oz (225 g) sieved cooked potato then bind with the milk. You will need approximately 7½ fl oz (225 ml). Continue as for the main recipe.

**Oatmeal Soda Bread:** Use 12 oz (350 g) flour and 4 oz (115 g) rolled oats. Other ingredients are as the basic recipe.

## RICH VANILLA ICE CREAM

*Preparation time: 20 minutes*
*Cooking time: 15 minutes*
*Freezing time: 1–1½ hours*
*Quantity: 4–6 helpings*

This recipe has a combination of the 'cream' made with butter or margarine and milk and whipped evaporated milk. This gave the nearest approach possible in 1949 to real cream ices.

In that era most advice stated that the refrigerator should be set to the coldest position 30 minutes before placing the mixture in the freezing compartment and that it should stay in this position during freezing. After the mixture was frozen, the indicator should be returned to the normal position. This advice is no longer considered essential, although the quicker ices are frozen, the better the result.

**For the 'cream':**
2 oz (50 g) unsalted butter
¼ pint (150 ml) fresh milk

**For the ice cream:**
cream' made with the above
   ingredients
1 x 14 oz (400 g) can evaporated
   milk, whipped (see right)
1 teaspoon vanilla essence
2 oz (50 g) icing or caster sugar

To make the cream, heat the butter and milk until just warm then allow to cool. To prevent the butter and milk separating as they cool, tip the mixture from the pan into a bowl and back again several times. When cold, pump vigorously through the cream-maker then chill.

Fold the cream into the whipped evaporated milk with the vanilla essence and sugar. Icing sugar should be sifted before using. Pour into the freezing trays of the refrigerator or a suitable container. Freeze until firm. This recipe does not need whipping during freezing.

### VARIATIONS

**Without the 'Cream':** Use just the whipped evaporated milk, add vanilla essence and the sugar, which could be reduced to 1½ oz (40 g). This mixture could be used as a basis for the following three ice creams instead of the Rich Vanilla Ice Cream.

**Brown Bread Ice Cream:** Fold 2–3 oz (50–85 g) fine soft or crisp

## ECONOMICAL ICE CREAMS

As cream was still unobtainable, all ice creams had to be based on substitutes, particularly evaporated milk, which was obtainable on the points system. 'Cream' made with a cream-making machine was rather too solid for a good texture, but you could mix some of this with evaporated milk, as in Rich Vanilla Ice Cream, left. In order to get a smooth mixture one needed a fairly high percentage of fat, so canned evaporated milk had to be used undiluted. The best result was obtained by whipping the evaporated milk, which made it a better colour and texture. Whipping evaporated milk is quite a long process. First, put the unopened can into a saucepan of water, making sure the can is completely immersed. Allow the water to boil for 15 minutes. Check from time to time that there is sufficient water, adding more boiling water, if necessary. Remove the can from the water and chill for some hours. Open the can, pour the milk into a large bowl and whisk until light and fluffy.
An even better texture is given by carefully opening the can after 15 minutes' boiling, pouring the hot milk into a container then adding 1 teaspoon gelatine, dissolved in 2 tablespoons water. Chill well for some hours then whip.
The recipes on this page are based upon 1 x 14 oz (400 g) can of evaporated milk, whipped with, or without, the gelatine.

brown breadcrumbs into the mixture. Use brown sugar, if possible, instead of white. The vanilla essence could be omitted and 1–2 tablespoons rum added.

**Custard Ice Cream:** Follow the recipe above and combine it with ½ pint (300 ml) thick custard, made with custard powder or 2 reconstituted dried eggs (see page 10) or fresh eggs, ½ pint (300 ml) fresh milk and 1 oz (25 g) sugar. This is a children's favourite. Because of the higher liquid content, it is improved by beating briskly halfway through freezing.

**Fruit Ice Cream:** Add 7 fl oz (225 ml) unsweetened smooth fruit purée to the whipped evaporated milk with 2½ oz (65 g) sugar or 10 fl oz (300 ml) to the Rich Vanilla Ice Cream with 3 oz (85 g) sugar.

**Fudge Ice Cream:** Omit additional sugar in this recipe. Melt 3–4 oz (85–115 g) fudge in a basin over hot water. Allow to cool then blend with the other ingredients. Vanilla essence can be added but is not essential.

**A MODERN TOUCH**
Use whipped whipping cream or double cream instead of the evaporated milk and cream.

☆ ☆ ☆ ☆ ☆ ☆ ☆ ☆ ☆ ☆ ☆ ☆ ☆ ☆ ☆ ☆ ☆ ☆ ☆ ☆ ☆ ☆ ☆ ☆ ☆

# SORBETS AND WATER ICES

The ices of 1949 were very simple compared with the more sophisticated recipes of the future. In large houses sorbets had been made in the years before the war as a course in the menu of formal banquets. The mixture would have been aerated by the use of an old-fashioned ice cream maker, where someone had the laborious task of turning the handle. Few people had these in their homes and the modern electric ones were many years ahead. The sorbets of 1949 were made lighter by the use of gelatine and egg whites. Fresh eggs were still on ration but people living in the country and those who kept chickens were able to use them. There were no fears in 1949 about using uncooked eggs.

☆ ☆ ☆ ☆ ☆ ☆ ☆ ☆ ☆ ☆ ☆ ☆ ☆ ☆ ☆ ☆ ☆ ☆ ☆ ☆ ☆ ☆ ☆ ☆ ☆

## Fruit Sorbets

Make 1 pint (600 ml) smooth fruit purée, either by liquidizing fresh or cooked fruit or rubbing it through a sieve to get rid of all pips and skin.

Sprinkle 2 level teaspoons gelatine on to 4 tablespoons water, stand for 3 minutes then dissolve over a pan of hot water.

Heat ¼ pint (150 ml) water with 2 oz (50 g) sugar until the sugar has dissolved. Add 2 tablespoons lemon juice, then mix in the dissolved gelatine. Add to the fruit purée and freeze until mushy.

Whisk 2 egg whites until stiff then fold into the fruit mixture and continue freezing.

## Water Ices

Use the recipe on the left, but omit the gelatine and egg whites. Freeze until firm. Always remove from the freezing compartment of the refrigerator about 15 minutes before serving.

## Sundaes

Restaurants began to serve sundaes as desserts and people at home decided to copy them. As fresh cream was still unobtainable, most people omitted a cream topping, although Mock Cream (see page 71) could be used.

## Peach Melba

Spoon ice cream into sundae glasses. Top with halved, skinned fresh or well-drained canned peach halves. Top with Melba Sauce.

For Melba Sauce, put 8 oz (225 g) fresh raspberries into a saucepan. Blend 1 level teaspoon arrowroot or cornflour with 3 tablespoons water and add to the pan with 3 tablespoons redcurrant jelly. Stir over a low heat until the mixture has thickened and become clear. Sieve or put into a liquidizer (blender). Processing in a liquidizer does not get rid of all the pips.

When fresh raspberries are unavailable use canned and 3 tablespoons liquid from the can to blend with the arrowroot or cornflour.

## Coupe Jacques

Spoon ice cream into sundae glasses, top with a fresh or well-drained canned fruit salad and Melba Sauce (Peach Melba, above).

## Poires Belle Hélène

Spoon ice cream into sundae glasses, top with peeled fresh or well-drained pear halves and Chocolate Sauce.

For Chocolate Sauce, put 2 oz (50 g) butter or margarine into a saucepan with 2 oz (50 g) caster sugar, 2 level tablespoons golden syrup, 4 tablespoons water and 2 oz (50 g) cocoa powder or chocolate powder for a milder taste.

Stir over the heat until the ingredients have melted. If serving cold, add an extra tablespoon water.

---

## JAM SAUCES

Preserves were taken off the ration at the end of 1948, so by 1949 people were buying generous amounts to make sauces to serve with steamed puddings. The recipes below give 4 good helpings.

### Jam Sauce

Put 6–8 tablespoons jam into a saucepan. Blend 1 level teaspoon arrowroot or cornflour with ¼ pint (150 ml) cold water, add to the pan and stir over a moderate heat until the mixture boils and becomes clear. To give more flavour to the sauce add 1 tablespoon lemon juice.

### Redcurrant Sauce

This is a lovely clear sauce, without thickening, which is ideal for spooning over puddings and ice cream.

Put 8 tablespoons redcurrant jelly and 3 tablespoons water into a saucepan. Stir over a low heat until the jelly has dissolved. Use hot.

If using the sauce cold, increase the amount of water to 5 tablespoons so the sauce does not become too thick.

# ★1950★

THE NEW HOUSE OF COMMONS was opened by King George VI in October. The old building had been severely damaged in an air raid in 1941.

Newspapers reported a French plan for a European Federation. The idea was originally to control coal and steel production in France and Germany. The organization would be open to other European states, including Russia, and further projects were envisaged.

British troops left Hong Kong in the summer to aid the Americans fighting in South Korea. Throughout the subsequent months there were worrying reports of severe action.

Information about the increases in teachers' salaries showed there was still a large differential between the amounts paid to men and women in this profession.

A supermarket where the customers walked around and selected their own goods was a big contrast to shopping locally. Most people deposited their ration coupons with their grocer and butcher. This meant it was difficult to buy rationed foods, such as fats, sugar, tea and meat at other shops. There were however, more unrationed foods available.

Sainsbury's opened their first self-service store in Croydon. The first credit cards were launched by Diner's Club.

The BBC transmitted a television picture to France in August. This was the first time such an event had happened. The sale of television sets increased by 250 per cent during the year and this was reflected in the heavy postbag received from viewers about all kinds of cookery matters. Some people wanted recipes from abroad, an interest reflected in articles published during the year in the Ministry of Food's *Food and Nutrition*. Information was given about the way people lived in various parts of the world, including such far-away places as Papua. An article on Indonesia went into some detail about the value of soya beans and soya milk.

Such articles did not detract from the Ministry's prime objective, which was to stress the importance of good nutrition. In order to make sure young people were eating wisely, the Ministry launched a film entitled *Feeding the under 20s*. The Ministry of Food's excellent *A.B.C. of Preserving* was published this year. It was sold at 6d (2½ p) by Her Majesty's Stationery Office.

British cooks had never used much oil in cooking, but in the June issue of *Food and Nutrition* there was a lengthy article about different kinds of oil – a portent, perhaps, for the years to come.

Ice cream was becoming Britain's favourite dessert and between-meal snack, though people did not have to make their own, unless they wished to. In 1939, annual ice cream sales in Britain were estimated to amount to £6,000,000. In 1940 the manufacture of ice cream had ceased, although a little was produced in the later years of the war to boost morale. By 1950, sales of ice cream had reached £14,000,000.

The commercial ice cream of this era was not of good quality, due to the shortage of basic ingredients. The public complained that it seemed 'full of air'. This was possibly true for the product was aerated to a great degree during manufacture.

# USING A LIQUIDIZER

By 1950, the number of people who had bought
liquidizers (blenders) had risen enormously,
so I was asked to give a number of
demonstrations on using them.
Liquidizers made simple work of producing
smooth purées of vegetables, fruit and other
ingredients. One lesson we had to stress in
demonstrations was that the goblet should
not be too full, for the mixture rises quite
dramatically, and the lid should be firmly placed,
or even held, in position when switching on.
In spite of this, people reported being showered
with soup or other liquid mixtures
because they failed to do this.
The liquidizer could only deal with small
amounts of solid foods at one time.
Food processors were unknown in 1950.

## HAM AND TOMATO PÂTÉ

Skin, deseed and chop 3 medium
tomatoes. Dice 5 oz (150 g) lean ham.
Put half the ingredients with a little
made mustard and a shake of pepper
into the liquidizer goblet, place the lid
in position, switch on and process
until smooth. Carefully remove the
purée and repeat with the remaining
ingredients.

### VARIATIONS

Add 1 or 2 spring onions or pickled
cocktail onions.

Use cooked chicken or 3 hard-
boiled eggs instead of ham; season
well.

Use lightly cooked liver instead
of ham, season well and add a pinch
of sugar.

Use smoked or cooked fresh
cod's roe instead of ham with seasoning and a squeeze of lemon juice.

## RABBIT PÂTÉ

*Preparation time: 30 minutes*
*Cooking time: 1½ hours*
*Quantity: 6 helpings*

Rabbits, which had been a valuable
part of family fare in the country during the war years, began to appear in
towns to be cooked in various ways.
This recipe adds a touch of luxury to
meals as a first course, or it makes an
excellent main dish with salad.

1 medium rabbit
3 bacon rashers
good pinch ground cinnamon
2 reconstituted dried eggs
   (see page 10) or fresh eggs
salt and pepper
1 tablespoon chopped mixed
   herbs or 1 teaspoon mixed
   dried herbs
2 tablespoons port wine

Take the liver, heart and kidney from
the rabbit. Put these, with the derinded bacon, through a mincer. Mix with
the cinnamon, one of the eggs and a
little seasoning.

Cut all the flesh from the bones of
the rabbit, and put through a mincer.

Add the herbs, the second egg and
port wine, season well. Spoon half the
minced bacon mixture into the base of
a small casserole, add the rabbit flesh
then cover with the remainder of the
minced bacon mixture. Press down
firmly with the back of a wooden
spoon. Cover tightly. Stand in a roast-
ing tin half-filled with water (this

stops the pâté drying in cooking).

Cook in a preheated oven set
to 160°C (325°F), Gas Mark 3 for
1½ hours.

When cooked, carefully remove
the casserole lid, put a plate with a
light weight on it on top of the pâté.
Leave the pâté until cold, then turn
out of the dish.

It's only a graze . . . but look at the dirt !

Lucky I've got MILTON —
that'll stop the germs and help it to heal!

## SPEEDY TOMATO SOUP

*Preparation time: 10 minutes*
*Cooking time: 5 minutes*
*Quantity: 4–6 helpings*

The liquidizer did not remove all the skins and pips from tomatoes but most people did not mind that. If one wanted the soup to be absolutely clear, the ingredients needed to be sieved after liquidizing or cooking, or the tomatoes concassed (the skins and seeds removed) before liquidizing. The flavour of this soup is delicious, as the cooking time is so short. It is also good served as a chilled soup without any cooking.

At first we were inclined to use ordinary British (strongly flavoured) onions, instead of the milder spring onions or shallots but if liquidized before cooking they retained a rather biting taste.

> 1 lb (450 g) tomatoes, chopped
> 1 small bunch spring onions or
>   2 shallots, chopped
> ½ small dessert apple, peeled
>   and chopped
> ¾ pint (450 ml) water or
>   chicken stock
> salt and pepper
> 1 teaspoon sugar
> 1 small sprig parsley
> few thyme leaves or pinch dried
>   thyme (optional)

There are too many ingredients in this recipe to liquidize all at once so put half the ingredients into the liquidizer goblet, place the lid in position then switch on. Tip the liquidized ingredients into a saucepan and repeat the liquidizing process with the remaining ingredients.

Cook the soup for 5 minutes only and serve.

### MODERN TOUCHES

A tablespoonful of tomato purée intensifies the flavour. A few basil leaves, a herb little known in the 1950s, can be used instead of the thyme. Milder red or sweet onions are excellent in this soup.

## LIQUIDIZERS AND OTHER APPLIANCES

In 1950 I gave a number of demonstrations using liquidizers and electric mixers due to the rise in their demand. It was not necessary to have special recipes for a mixer but what was essential was to use the machine correctly for each cooking purpose. I have included several of the recipes I used at these demonstrations in this chapter. There was not room to have a range of appliances in use in the Food Advice Bureau in the Harrods Food Hall. For many years this had been the Ministry of Food Bureau but towards the end of the 1940s its name was changed to Harrods Food Advice Bureau.

With the assistance of other home economists, I gave demonstrations each morning and afternoon to give the public the best help with their cookery problems and to suggest new and exciting dishes that could be made on the still meagre rations, plus the welcome unrationed foods arriving in Britain. At the beginning of 1950 I was asked to be responsible for a second bureau as well Harrods Home Service. This enabled me, with my assistants, to gave demonstrations of liquidizers, mixers, pressure cookers and other appliances, including exciting new washing machines, ironers and refrigerators.

## GRILLED PIGEONS

During this year the producer of the well-known and popular radio series *The Archers* came to Alexandra Palace, the home of BBC Television at that time, to ask me to demonstrate recipes using pigeons. The birds were causing much damage to crops at a time when it was essential that farmers produced as much wheat and corn as possible. Pigeons for grilling must be very young, often they are known as squabs. Allow 1 pigeon for each person. Wash and dry the birds and split lengthways. Season, then brush the birds with a generous amount of melted fat.

Preheat the grill and place the birds with the skin side uppermost on the grill pan. Cook for 5 minutes. Turn over and brush the under side with more fat. Continue cooking for a further 5 minutes. Turn the birds once more and cook until tender. To give more flavour to the flesh a few chopped herbs, such as parsley, thyme or rosemary, can be mixed with the melted fat. Serve the pigeons with redcurrant or apple jelly.

## PIGEON RAGOÛT

*Preparation time: 25 minutes*
*Cooking time: 1½ hours*
*Quantity: 4 helpings*

This is an excellent dish to make in summertime when tomatoes and cherries are in season.

1 oz (25 g) flour
salt and pepper
2 large or 4 small pigeons, halved
2 oz (50 g) dripping or cooking fat
4 small onions or bunch spring onions, sliced
4 small tomatoes, sliced
¾ pint (450 ml) brown stock
4–5 oz (115–150g) ripe cherries

Blend the flour with a generous amount of seasoning and coat the pigeons. Heat the dripping or fat in a pan, add the pigeons and cook gently for 10 minutes, turning over once or twice. Lift out of the pan and place in a casserole.

Add the onions and tomatoes to the pan and cook for 3 minutes then spoon over the pigeons. Pour the stock into the pan, stir well to absorb the meat juices and then pour into the casserole. Cover tightly.

Preheat the oven to 160°C (325°F), Gas Mark 3 and cook the casserole for 45 minutes. Add the cherries (which can be stoned first) and continue cooking for a further 30 minutes.

### VARIATION

Use a little less stock and add a few tablespoons of port wine to the other ingredients in the casserole.

Jelly tablets and crystals were now easily obtainable. For many people these were simpler to use than gelatine. The recipe on the right turns an ordinary lemon jelly into a delicious sweet.

### APRICOT AND LEMON JELLY

Make ½ pint (300 ml) smooth apricot purée by processing in the liquidizer cooked or canned apricots with a little of the syrup from cooking or canning. Make a jelly with ½ pint (300 ml) water, as instructed on the packet. Add the apricot purée. Pour into a mould and leave until firm. Turn out and decorate with Mock Cream (see page 71) and blanched almonds.

### VARIATIONS

Use canned pineapple or peaches instead of apricots. Fresh pineapple should never be added to any form of gelatine for it prevents the jelly from setting. The only solution is to cook the pineapple first.

Use a purée of uncooked raspberries with a raspberry jelly. A liquidizer does not get rid of all the pips so the purée needs to be rubbed through a sieve.

✩ ✩ ✩ ✩ ✩ ✩ ✩ ✩ ✩ ✩ ✩ ✩ ✩ ✩ ✩ ✩ ✩ ✩ ✩ ✩ ✩ ✩ ✩ ✩ ✩

## RETURN OF DRIED FRUITS

Although limited supplies of dried fruit were available on the points system throughout the years of rationing, it was a joy to have a really wide choice of the fruits free from restrictions. They enabled us to make some interesting dishes.

✩ ✩ ✩ ✩ ✩ ✩ ✩ ✩ ✩ ✩ ✩ ✩ ✩ ✩ ✩ ✩ ✩ ✩ ✩ ✩ ✩ ✩ ✩ ✩ ✩

### ORIENTAL FINGERS

*Preparation time: 25 minutes*
*Cooking time: 25–30 minutes*
*Quantity: 6–8 helpings*

**For the filling:**
2 oz (50 g) glacé cherries
2 oz (50 g) blanched almonds
  or other nuts
2 oz (50 g) dates, weight
  without stones
1 oz (50 g) sultanas
1 oz (25 g) butter or margarine
1 oz (25 g) caster or light
  brown sugar

**For the sweet shortcrust pastry:**
8 oz (225 g) plain flour
4 oz (115 g) butter or margarine
2 oz (50 g) caster sugar
little milk to bind

**For the topping:**
little icing sugar

Chop the cherries, nuts and dates for the filling into small pieces. Put into a saucepan with the rest of the filling ingredients and stir over a low heat until the fat and sugar have melted. Leave the mixture until cold.

Preheat the oven to 190°C (375°F), Gas Mark 5.

Sift the flour into a mixing bowl or the bowl of an electric mixer, add the butter or margarine and rub in by hand, or switch on the mixer, until the consistency of fine breadcrumbs. Do not over-handle. Add the sugar and gather the dough together. Gradually add sufficient milk to make a dough with a firm rolling consistency.

Divide the mixture into two equal portions and roll both out to oblongs about ¼ inch (6 mm) thick. Place one on an ungreased baking tray. Cover with the filling and then with the second sheet of pastry. Seal the edges lightly. Bake for 20–30 minutes until pale golden in colour and firm. Cool on the tray. When cold, cut into squares or fingers. Dust with sifted icing sugar.

### DATE AND WALNUT BARS

*Preparation time: 25 minutes*
*Cooking time: 25–30 minutes*
*Quantity: 12 cakes*

Various kinds of fresh nuts came back into the shops fairly soon after the war and dried nuts, used in this recipe, arrived at about the same time. In those days ready-cut candied (often called crystallized) peel was not available; you had to remove large lumps of sugar and chop the peel. Sugar was still regarded as a precious commodity so the pieces removed would be used to sweeten fruit.

4 oz (115 g) cooking dates
2 oz (50 g) walnuts
2 oz (50 g) glacé cherries
2 oz (50 g) mixed candied peel
4 oz (115 g) self-raising flour or
  plain flour with 1 teaspoon
  baking powder
2 oz (50 g) margarine
2 oz (50 g) sugar, preferably
  light brown
1 egg

Grease and flour an 8 inch (20 cm) square tin. Preheat the oven to 190°C (375°F), Gas Mark 5. Chop the dates, walnuts, cherries and peel.

Sift the flour, or flour and baking powder, into a bowl. Rub in the margarine, add the sugar then the rest of the ingredients. Spoon into the tin. Bake for 15 minutes or until brown, then reduce the oven temperature to 180°C (350°F), Gas Mark 4 and cook for a further 10–15 minutes, or until firm. Cut into portions while still warm, then remove from the tin.

The reason I'm glad
And my smile's so bright
You see on my tray
The food is just right

MINDER STOKEN
KORTER KOKEN
DAN BEHOUDT GE
GEUR EN SMAAK

EET IEDERE DAG GROENTE

A Good Breakfast

## CONGRESS TARTS

*Preparation time: 25 minutes*
*Cooking time: 20 minutes*
*Quantity: 9–12 tartlets*

When ground almonds came back on the market I had many enquiries about how to make real marzipan or almond paste and requests for recipes such as this one. I had demonstrated Mock Congress Tarts many times in the war years using semolina or fine breadcrumbs, with almond essence and lemon squash to give a semblance of the correct flavours.

**For the shortcrust or sweet shortcrust pastry:**
6 oz (175 g) flour, etc.
   (see Gypsy Tart, page 21, or
   Oriental Fingers, page 67)

**For the filling:**
little jam
2 oz (50 g) butter or margarine
2 oz (50 g) caster sugar
$\frac{1}{2}$-1 teaspoon finely grated
   lemon zest
1 egg
1 tablespoon lemon juice
2 oz (50 g) ground almonds

**To decorate:**
9–12 blanched almonds

Make the pastry as on pages 21 or 67. Preheat the oven to 190–200°C (375–400°F), Gas Mark 5–6. Use the higher setting for shallow tartlets and the lower one for deeper tarts.

Roll out the pastry and line 9–12 patty tins. Put a teaspoon of jam into each pastry case.

Cream the butter or margarine with the sugar and lemon zest. Beat the egg with the lemon juice and add to the creamed mixture together with the ground almonds. Spoon over the jam, top with an almond and bake for 15–20 minutes.

**VARIATION**
Omit the almonds when baking the tarts. Top with Lemon Icing (see Lemon Sponge, page 86) and the almonds.

## BABAS AU RHUM

*Preparation time: 25 minutes plus time for proving*
*Cooking time: 10–15 minutes*
*Quantity: 8–10 cakes or 12–14 smaller ones*

Cooking with yeast had become so popular with my audiences at Harrods that every Friday afternoon I gave a baking demonstration and included some kind of yeast recipe. These light yeast cakes were a great favourite. Rum was easily obtainable by 1950.

$\frac{1}{2}$ oz (15 g) fresh yeast or $\frac{1}{4}$ oz (7 g) dried yeast, (see comments on yeast, Home-made Bread, page 28)
$\frac{1}{4}$ pint (150 ml) milk or milk and water
2 oz (50 g) caster sugar
8 oz (225 g) plain flour
pinch salt
2 eggs
$\frac{1}{2}$ teaspoon vanilla essence
2 oz (50 g) butter or margarine, softened

**For the syrup:**
4 tablespoons water
4 tablespoons sugar or honey
squeeze lemon juice
3–5 tablespoons rum

**To decorate:**
Mock Cream (see page 71)
glacé cherries

Cream the fresh yeast in a basin. Warm the milk, or milk and water, add to the yeast and blend well. If using dried yeast add this to the warm milk with a teaspoon of the sugar. Sprinkle a little flour on top of the liquid. Leave until bubbles form.

Sift the flour with the salt into a mixing bowl, then add the rest of the sugar. Make a well in the centre and add the yeast liquid. Beat the eggs with the vanilla essence, add to the dough and mix very well. The mixture is too soft for kneading but it should be beaten well with a wooden spoon or the dough hook of an electric mixer, using a slow speed. Stop when the mixture looks smooth.

Place the softened butter or margarine over the dough, do not mix it in at this stage. Cover and leave in a warm place to prove for about 35 minutes or at room temperature for about 45–50 minutes. The dough should become almost double its original size.

Blend in the softened butter or margarine and beat again with a spoon or the dough hook. Grease 8–10 individual flan tins; if these are not available, use 12–14 castle pudding tins. Half fill with the dough and allow to prove for 15–20 minutes. Preheat the oven to 220°C (425°F), Gas Mark 7. Bake the larger cakes for about 15 minutes and the smaller ones for 10 minutes, or until just firm. Turn out on to a dish.

For the syrup, heat the water with the sugar or honey and lemon juice, add the rum. Prick the hot cakes with a fine skewer and spoon the hot syrup over them. When cold, decorate with Mock Cream and glacé cherries.

**VARIATIONS**
**Savarin:** Put the dough into a well-greased 8 inch (20 cm) ovenproof ring mould. Prove then bake for 20–25 minutes. If necessary, reduce the oven temperature to 190°C (375°F), Gas Mark 5 after 10–15 minutes. Soak with the syrup as before. This cake is delicious filled with fresh fruit salad and served as a dessert.

2–3 tablespoons of currants could be added to the dough in both recipes.

In 1950 the Communists from North Korea invaded independent South Korea. The
invasion took place without any prior warning. The United States of America
offered military aid to South Korea and the United Nations backed
any opposition to the Communists.
A number of British naval ships were already in the area and these were
placed under the command of the American General Douglas MacArthur.
The first British troops arrived in South Korea at the end of August.
They consisted of men from Scottish and Middlesex regiments.
Later in 1950 the Chinese entered the war on the side
of the North Koreans.

✩ ✩ ✩ ✩ ✩ ✩ ✩ ✩ ✩ ✩ ✩ ✩ ✩ ✩ ✩ ✩ ✩ ✩ ✩ ✩ ✩ ✩ ✩ ✩ ✩ ✩

## MOCK CREAM

People had become used to making mock cream in various ways. Since few homes possessed a cream-making machine, this recipe had become the favourite way of producing an acceptable substitute for real cream.
Blend 1 level tablespoon cornflour with ¼ pint (150 ml) milk. Tip into a saucepan and stir carefully over a low heat until the mixture becomes very thick. Pour into a basin, cover to prevent a skin forming, and leave until cold.
Cream 1 oz (25 g) butter or margarine (it is worthwhile using butter if you can spare it) with ½–1 oz (15–25 g) caster or sifted icing sugar. Very gradually beat teaspoons of the cornflour mixture into the creamed fat and sugar. An electric mixer does this very efficiently but whether mixing by hand or by machine, the secret is to incorporate the cornflour mixture slowly and beat hard.
For a less thick cream use 7½ fl oz (225 ml) milk.
To make a thick cream, follow the method given but use 4 oz (115 g) butter to the 7½ fl oz (225 ml) milk.
There is a recipe for making a pouring cream with a machine on page 59 (Rich Vanilla Ice Cream).

✩ ✩ ✩ ✩ ✩ ✩ ✩ ✩ ✩ ✩ ✩ ✩ ✩ ✩ ✩ ✩ ✩ ✩ ✩ ✩ ✩ ✩ ✩ ✩ ✩ ✩

## Egg Nog

This was a favourite drink when liquidizers were first introduced. Manufacturer's would demonstrate the machine using the egg in its shell. I doubt whether many people did the same thing in their own home. This was a recipe where reconstituted dried egg did not give a particularly good flavour, it had to be a fresh egg.

Put a fresh egg with 1–2 teaspoons sugar and ½ pint (300 ml) milk into the goblet. Add 2–3 tablespoons brandy or whisky. Cover and switch on. Serve cold or heat for just 1 minute, taking care the mixture does not boil.

## FRUIT MILK SHAKE

Put a spoonful of crushed ice or ice cream into the liquidizer goblet. Add a small or ½ large sliced banana or a few strawberries or other fruit and a good ½ tumbler of milk. Cover and switch on until smooth and frothy.
NOTE: It is essential that the ice is crushed, as otherwise it would damage the blades of the liquidizer. Put the ice cubes on to a clean teacloth, cover with the cloth and crush with a rolling pin.

# ★1951★

I N MAY THE Festival of Britain was opened by the King and Queen. It was created on 27 acres of bomb-damaged land on the south side of the Thames. The idea was to combine fun and fantasy in the Pleasure Gardens of Battersea Park; the objective of the Government-sponsored Festival was to show the world that, in spite of the present austerity, Britain was looking forward to a much brighter future. To make certain that all the refreshments sold at the Festival were as good as possible, a committee of people in the food world were asked to visit the Festival regularly and check on the food and drink. I was a member of the committee.

The King also opened Festival Hall.

The election held in this year brought the Conservatives back into power, with Winston Churchill as Prime Minister once again.

The survey of the time spent in the home by most housewives established that, on average, they worked 75 hours a week, with overtime on Saturdays and Sundays. This did not take into account that a number of women were also doing part or full-time work outside the home.

Tuppence (2d) was taken off the meat ration at the beginning of the year. This meant that the average weekly ration was now about 4 oz (115 g), the lowest it had been. Butchers estimated that, with rising prices, it would take the meat coupons from 3 ration books to buy 1 lb (450 g) meat a week.

One good thing was that chickens, rabbits and pigeons were more readily available. Rice was also available again, after some years of shortages.

Some interesting fruits and vegetables, such as avocados, red and green peppers and aubergines, were becoming more generally known. I tried to take a rather unusual fruit or vegetable to each television programme and explain just how to serve it.

The number of refrigerators on sale in Britain was increasing and various firms were advertising their models quite extensively. Cream was still unobtainable, so I made various ice creams in one of my television programmes using the recipes for Economical Ice Creams in the 1949 chapter (see page 59).

The range of subjects that readers of magazines and viewers of television wanted to have discussed was very varied. Young men and women, many of whom had gone straight from school into the forces, had not had a chance to learn to cook basic meals in their own homes. Now, they wanted to learn basic principles and know how to choose food, such as vegetables and fish, wisely. While the allowance of meat was so low there was little point in dealing with a selection of cuts of meat; that had to wait until after the summer of 1954.

Older people thought nostalgically of our traditional recipes from before the war and wanted these shown on television. None of these requests was easy to fulfil, due to the strict rationing still in force.

Television in these days was such a personal medium. People wrote copious letters to all who appeared before the cameras. The viewers felt they knew you well and could write and comment on the programme and also on the dress you wore and the way you had your hair.

# HOW YOU FEEL TOMORROW
## *depends a lot on*
# TODAY...

## FISH PILAFF

*Preparation time: 20 minutes*
*Cooking time: 30 minutes*
*Quantity: 4 helpings*

This mixture of rice, fish and other ingredients makes a very satisfying and easily prepared meal.

1 lb (450 g) white fish, skinned
2 oz (50 g) margarine
2 medium onions, chopped
1 garlic clove, crushed (optional)
6 oz (175 g) long-grain rice
1 pint (600 ml) water
salt and pepper

2 medium tomatoes, skinned and chopped
2 oz (50 g) raisins

Cut the fish into 1 inch (2.5 cm) dice, removing any bones. Heat half the margarine in a large saucepan, add the fish and cook carefully for 5 minutes until slightly brown and nearly tender. Remove from the pan with a fish slice and place on a plate.

Heat the remaining margarine in the same pan, add the onions and garlic, if using, and cook for 5 minutes. Put in the rice and stir until it is well blended with the onions. Add the water, bring to the boil, season well, then lower the heat. Cover the pan and cook for 10 minutes. Stir well, then put in the tomatoes and raisins. Cook for a further 5 minutes, stir once more, then add the fish. Continue cooking until the rice is tender, the fish is very hot and any excess liquid has evaporated. The dish should be moist but not too wet. Serve with mixed vegetables.

## CHICKEN BROTH

*Preparation time: 20 minutes*
*Cooking time: 1½ hours*
*Quantity: 4 helpings*

bones from a chicken
3 onions
3 carrots
2 celery sticks
salt and pepper
1¼ pints (750 ml) chicken stock (see method)
1½ oz (40 g) long-grain rice
few canned or cooked peas or beans, if available
½ pint (300 ml) milk

**To garnish:**
diced toast
chopped parsley

Break the bones of the chicken with a small weight. This makes it easier to extract the flavour. Put the bones into a saucepan. Peel and roughly chop 1 onion, 1 carrot and the celery. Add to the bones with 2½ pints (1.5 litres) water and a little seasoning. Cover the pan and simmer for 1 hour.

Peel the remaining onions and carrots and cut into ½ inch (1.25 cm) dice. Strain the stock and measure out 1¼ pints (750 ml). Pour into a saucepan, bring to the boil, then add the rice and the diced vegetables. Cook steadily for 30 minutes, then add the peas and the milk. Simmer for another 5 minutes, then garnish and serve.

**VARIATIONS**
Make the stock in a pressure cooker. Allow only 30 minutes cooking time and use 1½ pints (900 ml) water: this is sufficient because the liquid does not evaporate as much in a pressure cooker as it does in a saucepan.

Save a little cooked chicken breast from the carcass and dice this neatly. Add to the soup with the milk.

## RED AND GREEN PEPPER SALAD

*Preparation time: 15 minutes*
*No cooking*
*Quantity: 4 helpings*

2 green peppers
1 red pepper
4 oz (115 g) Cheddar cheese, grated
2 tablespoons finely diced gherkins
2 large tomatoes, skinned and finely chopped
3 tablespoons mayonnaise
salt and pepper
lettuce

Cut a slice from the stalk end of the peppers and deseed them. Chop the slices and all the red pepper very finely. Mix with the cheese, gherkins, chopped tomatoes and mayonnaise. Spoon the mixture into the green peppers and chill for a time. Cut into slices and arrange on a bed of lettuce.

## SAVOURY CHEESE PIE

*Preparation time: 30 minutes*
*Cooking time: 40 minutes*
*Quantity: 4 helpings*

The small amount of meat available during 1951 meant that cheese was often used to make a main dish, such as in this pie, which is not unlike a filled quiche.

**For the savoury pastry:**
6 oz (175 g) plain flour
salt and pepper
½ teaspoon mustard powder
3 oz (85 g) margarine or
    cooking fat
1 oz (25 g) cheese, finely grated
1 tablespoon chopped parsley
water, to bind

**For the filling:**
1 oz (25 g) margarine
2 medium onions, chopped
2 medium cooked potatoes,
    diced
2 tomatoes, thinly sliced
2 eggs
¼ pint (150 ml) milk
1 tablespoon chopped parsley
2 oz (50 g) cheese, grated

To make the pastry, sift the flour with the seasonings, rub in the magarine or fat, add the cheese and parsley and enough water to make a pastry with a firm rolling consistency.

Wrap the pastry and chill briefly in the refrigerator then roll out and use to line an 8 inch (20 cm) shallow flan tin or dish. Preheat the oven to 190°C (375°F), Gas Mark 5 and heat a baking tray at the same time. Stand the baking tin or dish on the hot baking tray and cook the pastry case 'blind' for only 15 minutes (see page 47). Remove the pastry shell from the oven and lower the oven temperature to 160°C (325°F), Gas Mark 3.

While the pastry is cooking, make the filling. Heat the margarine, add the onions and cook gently for 8 minutes. Mix with the diced potatoes and put into the partially cooked pastry shell. Top with the sliced tomatoes. Beat the eggs, add the milk and the rest of the ingredients. Season to taste and pour over the potato mixture. Return the pie to the oven and bake for approximately 25 minutes, or until the filling is set. Serve hot or cold.

## MOUSSAKA

*Preparation time: 35 minutes*
*Cooking time: 1 hour 20 minutes*
*Quantity: 4 helpings*

2 medium aubergines,
    thinly sliced
salt and pepper
4 medium potatoes,
    thickly sliced
1½ oz (40 g) margarine or
    cooking fat
3 medium onions,
    thinly sliced
4 medium tomatoes,
    thickly sliced
8 oz (225 g) lamb, mutton
    or beef, minced

**For the sauce:**
1 oz (25 g) margarine
1 oz (25 g) flour
12 fl oz (350 ml) milk
1 egg
2–3 oz (50–85 g) cheese,
    grated
pinch grated or ground
    nutmeg

**To garnish:**
chopped parsley

Sprinkle the aubergine slices with a little salt, leave for about 20 minutes then drain and rinse in cold water. Dry well. This draws out the slightly bitter taste from the skins. Put the aubergine and potato slices into a steamer over a pan of boiling water. Cover and steam for about 10 minutes or until just soft but not mushy.

Heat the margarine or cooking fat, add the onions and cook slowly for 5 minutes. Add the tomatoes and the meat, mix well and cook gently for another 10 minutes, stirring all the time.

For the sauce, heat the margarine, add the flour and then most of the milk. Stir over a moderate heat until the sauce thickens. Remove from the heat. Beat the egg with the remaining milk and whisk it into the hot sauce, together with half the cheese, seasoning and nutmeg.

Arrange layers of the onion and meat mixture and the aubergines and potatoes in a casserole. Spread a little sauce over each layer. End with a potato and aubergine layer and the last of the sauce then top with the remaining cheese. Bake for 1 hour in a preheated oven set to 160°C (325°F), Gas Mark 3. Top with parsley and serve hot.

**A MODERN TOUCH**
There is no need to salt the aubergines today.

## AVOCADO AND ORANGE COCKTAIL

*Preparation time: 10 minutes*
*No cooking*
*Quantity: 4 helpings*

Avocados were becoming better known. The partnership of avocados and oranges makes a perfect start to a meal.

**For the dressing:**
3 tablespoons olive oil
1 tablespoon lemon juice
   or white wine vinegar
salt and pepper
2 oranges
2 ripe avocados
lettuce heart

Mix together the oil, lemon juice or vinegar and seasoning. Cut away the peel and pith from the oranges then, working over a basin so no juice is wasted, cut out the orange segments. Remove any pips or skin. Add a little of the orange juice to the dressing. Any juice left can be put into a fruit salad. Halve, stone and skin the avocados and cut the flesh into neat dice. Put into the dressing with the orange segments.

Shred the lettuce finely, put into individual glasses then top with the avocado mixture and dressing. Chill well for a short time before serving.

**VARIATION**
Use grapefruit segments instead of orange or use a combination of orange and grapefruit.

## FRUITY RICE

*Preparation time: 15 minutes*
*Cooking time: 2 hours*
*Quantity: 4 helpings*

Rice was little used in Britain except for puddings or to accompany a curry, so the lack of rice in previous years had not been a great problem. Now rice had returned, people could make good puddings, although one or two people did try making a pilaff with long-grain rice.

2 oz (50 g) short-grain rice
1 pint (600 ml) milk
1 teaspoon finely grated
   lemon zest
2 teaspoons finely grated
   orange zest
2 oz (50 g) sugar, or to taste
3 tablespoons raisins
3 tablespoons sultanas

**For the topping:**
2 oranges
1 oz (25 g) sugar

Preheat the oven to 150°C (300°F), Gas Mark 2. Put all the ingredients for the pudding (but not the topping) into a 2 pint (1.2 litre) pie dish and bake for 1¾ hours.

Meanwhile, prepare the topping. Cut away the peel from the oranges then cut the fruit into thin rings, removing any pips. Take the pudding from the oven and arrange the orange rings over it. Sprinkle with sugar then return to the oven for 15 minutes. Serve hot.

## LEMON FLUMMERY

*Preparation time: 15 minutes*
*Cooking time: 10 minutes*
*Quantity: 4 helpings*

I had made this recipe during the war years, using the very oddly flavoured lemon squash then available: what a joy to be able to use real lemons.

½ teaspoon finely grated
   lemon zest
3 tablespoons lemon juice
cold water (see method)
2 oz (50 g) sugar
½ oz (15 g) gelatine
   (see note right)
2 reconstituted dried eggs
   (see page 10) or fresh eggs

Put the lemon zest, lemon juice and nearly all the water into a saucepan, add the sugar and heat gently for a few minutes to soften the zest and dissolve the sugar. Pour the remaining cold water into a basin, add the gelatine, allow to stand for 3 minutes then place over a saucepan of very hot water until dissolved. Stir into the lemon mixture and mix well. Take the pan off the heat and whisk in the well-beaten eggs.

Return the pan to the heat and simmer gently, whisking all the time, for 4–5 minutes. Pour the mixture into a rinsed mould and leave until firm then turn out.
NOTE: With modern gelatine, use 1 sachet, i.e. 0.4 oz (11 g).

The travelling salesman from Walls Ice Cream had been a feature on the roads before the war and it was a welcome sight to see him back again. There were also some women doing the same job.
The roads at that time were relatively quiet compared to modern day traffic, so that riding a bicycle and stopping frequently to sell ice cream was not the danger it would be today.

☆ ☆ ☆ ☆ ☆ ☆ ☆ ☆ ☆ ☆ ☆ ☆ ☆ ☆ ☆ ☆ ☆ ☆ ☆ ☆ ☆ ☆ ☆ ☆ ☆ ☆

## THE FESTIVAL OF BRITAIN

The Festival was opened by the King and Queen on 4 May 1951. This was 100 years after the Victorian Great Exhibition. A team of distinguished experts, led by Hugh Casson, the famous architect, created this Festival on what had previously been wasteland near Waterloo.
To quote the words used at the time:

'The whole of this large expanse was planned
to create a feeling of fun, fantasy and colour'.

The scene on the left shows the Festival in full swing. The Festival was sponsored by the Labour Government. One of the ministers, Herbert Morrison, described its purpose as 'the people giving themselves a pat on the back'.
Certainly the public flocked to the Festival where they could enjoy the various sights, the funfair and the pleasure gardens.
In addition to the Festival of Britain the new Festival Hall was opened. This provided a first class concert hall with modern amenities.

☆ ☆ ☆ ☆ ☆ ☆ ☆ ☆ ☆ ☆ ☆ ☆ ☆ ☆ ☆ ☆ ☆ ☆ ☆ ☆ ☆ ☆ ☆ ☆ ☆

### GINGER BUNS

*Preparation time:*
*5 minutes*
*Cooking time:*
*2–15 minutes*
*Quantity: 12 cakes*

1 oz (25 g) crystallized ginger
6 oz (175 g) self-raising flour or plain flour with 1½ teaspoons baking powder
1 oz (25 g) cornflour
1 teaspoon ground ginger, or to taste
pinch mixed spice
4 oz (115 g) margarine
4 oz (115 g) soft brown sugar
2 teaspoons golden syrup
1 egg
milk, to mix

Preheat the oven to 200°C (400°F), Gas Mark 6. Grease and flour 12 patty tins or place paper cases in the tins. Finely chop the crystallized ginger.

Sift the flour with the baking powder and spices. Cream the margarine, sugar and syrup until soft. Beat the egg, add to the mixture, then fold in the flour and enough milk to make a firm dropping consistency. Lastly add the crystallized ginger. Spoon the mixture into the tins or paper cases and bake until firm.

**VARIATION**
When cold, the cakes can be coated with a thin layer of ginger-flavoured icing (see Ginger Icing, page 86), and a thin slice of crystallized ginger.

## ECONOMICAL BOURBON BISCUITS

*Preparation time: 15 minutes*
*Cooking time: 10–12 minutes*
*Quantity: 15 complete biscuits*

3 oz (85 g) margarine
2 oz (50 g) caster sugar
2 level tablespoons
   golden syrup
few drops vanilla essence
6 oz (175 g) plain flour
1 oz (25 g) rice flour or
   fine semolina
1 oz (25 g) cocoa powder
few drops of milk,
   if necessary (see method)

**For Chocolate Butter
Icing:**

1½ oz (40 g) butter
   or margarine
2 teaspoons cocoa powder
2oz (50 g) icing sugar

Preheat the oven to 160°C (325°F), Gas Mark 3. Lightly grease two baking trays.

Cream the margarine, sugar, golden syrup and vanilla essence until soft and light. Sift the flour with the rice flour or semolina and cocoa powder into the creamed ingredients and knead very thoroughly. Try to avoid using any milk if possible, but the dough should be a firm rolling consistency.

Flour a pastry board very sparingly – you do not want a floury outside to these biscuits. Roll out the dough until it is just over ⅛ inch (3 mm) thick and cut into fingers about 1 inch (2.5 cm) wide and the required length.

Place the fingers on the baking tray and prick lightly at regular intervals. Bake for 10–12 minutes, or until just firm. Leave on the trays until cold.

Cream the butter or margarine for the icing, sift the icing sugar and cocoa into it and mix well. Sandwich the biscuits together with a little of the icing.

### VARIATIONS

The Chocolate Biscuit recipe on page 99 makes a richer biscuit.
**Chocolate Butter Icing 2:**
Supplies of icing sugar were still uncertain so you could make the filling without it by creaming together 1½ oz (40 g) butter or margarine, 1 level tablespoon golden syrup and 1½ oz (40 g) sifted chocolate or cocoa powder.

In this case chocolate powder (if available) makes a less strongly flavoured filling.

### REAL MARZIPAN

Mix together 4 oz (115 g) ground almonds with 2 oz (50 g) caster sugar, 2 oz (50 g) sifted icing sugar and a few drops of almond essence. Bind with the yolk of an egg.

### MARZIPAN BUNS

These would be a good cake for a children's party. They are based on the recipe for Home-made Bread (see page 28). Use the same ingredients as for Home-made Bread After the dough has proved in bulk, take off about half to make a loaf then use the remainder for these buns.

Make 12–15 round balls with the dough. Make a deep indentation in each of the balls with your finger and put a little marzipan inside (see above). Gently roll the dough again until the marzipan is completely enclosed.

Place the buns on a baking tray and allow to prove until almost double in size. Preheat the oven to 220°C (425°F), Gas Mark 7. Bake the buns for 12–15 minutes.

While the buns are still hot, brush them with a glaze made by dissolving 2 tablespoons sugar in 2 tablespoons hot water.

## CONTINENTAL FRUIT BREAD

*Preparation time: 30 minutes,*
*plus time for proving*
*Cooking time: 35–40 minutes*
*Quantity: 2 loaves*

This is a delicious bread to eat with butter when fresh. Slices can be toasted when the bread gets stale.

Use the ingredients for Home-made Bread (see page 28), but use ¾ oz (20 g) fresh yeast or 3 teaspoons dried yeast and decrease the water by 4 tablespoons

**Additional ingredients:**
2 oz (50 g) margarine or
  cooking fat
2 oz (50 g) sugar
1 teaspoon grated lemon zest
3 oz (85 g) sultanas
2 eggs

**For the topping:**
little milk
1 oz (25 g) chopped almonds

Sift the flour and salt for the bread into a mixing bowl. Rub in the margarine or cooking fat then add the sugar, lemon zest and sultanas. Cream fresh yeast or dissolve dried yeast (see Home-made Bread, page 28), add the warm water and beaten eggs then continue as in the method for Home-made Bread, allowing the dough to prove in bulk.

When it has proved, divide into four portions. Form two of these portions into oval shapes about 8 inch (20 cm) long and 4 inches (10 cm) wide. Cut each of the other two portions into three strips and plait them loosely. Place over the oval shapes. Brush with milk and sprinkle with almonds.

Allow to prove until nearly double in size. Bake the bread in a preheated ovenset to 200°C (400°F), Gas Mark 6 for 35–40 minutes.

# ★1952★

IN JANUARY NEWSPAPERS **and television carried pictures of the King and Queen saying farewell to Princess Elizabeth and Prince Philip at the start of their journey to Australia. They were going to stay in Kenya for a safari holiday en route.**

One week later the nation learned that George VI had died peacefully in his sleep. There was genuine grief throughout Britain and the Commonwealth, for the shy quiet man, who had never expected to be king, had earned everyone's respect and affection. It was a sad return to this country for his young daughter, who was now Queen Elizabeth II.

In November the Queen opened her first Parliament. By then, there was much talk about the new Elizabethan age and just what Britain would achieve under this Queen Elizabeth in the years to come.

In February tea came off ration and there was much rejoicing. We had always been a tea-drinking nation and the small amount allowed meant one never seemed to have sufficient to enjoy odd cups of tea. Over the years since 1940, when rationing began, people had developed ways to eke out the tea. If any tea was left in the teapot it was strained into a vacuum flask to be heated later. Many people used the tea leaves twice, the second brew was weak, but it still gave a warming drink.

Television had made people more aware of all sorts of sporting events, including tennis at Wimbledon. A competitor who endeared herself to the public was the American Maureen Connolly, known as Little Mo. She won the women's singles at her first attempt at the age of 17.

Little Mo went on to win the Wimbledon championship for a further two years.

The Duchess of Kent was a great supporter of Wimbledon and the Kent family still is.

Appliances that had been on sale for several years and had grown rapidly in popularity were electric mixers and liquidizers (often known as blenders). The mixer took away the hard work of creaming and other tasks and cooks were grateful for this. Some people were not entirely satisfied with the results of cake-making with an electric mixer and I had many letters from ladies who had made wonderful sponges and light cakes, indeed in some instances winning prizes before the war. Now, having saved their rations to repeat their success, they were disappointed at the results when using a mixer. I had to demonstrate that one must take time and learn how to reconcile the cookery techniques of hand-mixing to the use of an efficient electric appliance.

Liquidizers were a joy and in many cases the sieve, which was time-consuming and quite hard work to use and clean, was now superfluous. The liquidizer would give smooth purées of vegetables or fruits within seconds, so that soup-making and many desserts were now possible for busy people.

For several television programmes during the year I demonstrated invalid cookery. It was a fact that during the war years people had rarely complained about illnesses unless they were very serious. Now, people were very concerned with gastric problems and diets. Some of the recipes I gave on television are in this chapter.

By 1952, Bird's Eye had started quick-freezing peas at Lowestoft in Suffolk.

## GINGER NUTS

*Preparation time: 15 minutes*
*Cooking time: 15 minutes*
*Quantity: 15–18 biscuits*

The baking instructions for these biscuits may seem rather unusual but they give the best result. If the baked biscuits are not quite as crisp as you would wish, return them to the oven at the lower heat for a few more minutes.

2 oz (50 g) margarine or
   cooking fat
2 level tablespoons golden syrup
1 oz (25 g) light brown sugar
4 oz (115 g) plain flour
l level teaspoon bicarbonate
   of soda
½–1 teaspoon each of mixed
   spice, ground cinnamon
   and ground ginger

Preheat the oven to 200°C (400°F), Gas Mark 6. Grease two baking trays very well.

Melt the margarine or cooking fat with the syrup in a saucepan. Remove from the heat, and add the sugar. Sift the flour very thoroughly with the bicarbonate of soda and spices, add to the melted ingredients and mix well. If the mixture is a little sticky, allow it to stand in a cool place for at least 15 minutes. Roll into 15–18 small balls and place these on the trays, allowing space for them to spread.

Bake for 5 minutes, then immediately lower the oven temperature to 180°C (350°F), Gas Mark 4 and bake for a further 10 minutes. It helps the temperature in an electric oven to drop if the door is opened slightly until the setting is reached. Cool the biscuits on the trays. When cold, store in an airtight tin away from other biscuits.

### VARIATION

**Chocolate Nuts:** For this variation on the Ginger Nuts above, sift 3 oz (85 g) plain flour with 1 oz (25 g) cocoa powder and 1 level teaspoon bicarbonate of soda. Melt the fat and syrup as for Ginger Nuts, add the sugar and ¼ teaspoon vanilla essence. Add the dry ingredients, knead well then roll into balls. Bake as for Ginger Nuts. One of the three spices could be used in these biscuits, if liked.

☆ ☆ ☆ ☆ ☆ ☆ ☆ ☆ ☆ ☆ ☆ ☆ ☆ ☆ ☆ ☆ ☆ ☆ ☆ ☆ ☆ ☆ ☆ ☆ ☆

# COME TO TEA

People in Britain were tending to entertain quite a lot, in spite of the continued rationing of many foods. When the tea ration was abolished, I had a great many requests for more cake and biscuit recipes for special tea parties.

The cake and biscuit recipes most in demand were those that used fairly low quantities of fat and sugar. The Chocolate Gâteau recipe, below, is typical of the kind of special cake parents or grandparents made for their family or friends for a special occasion. They would have to use part of their precious sweet ration in the form of plain chocolate in order to produce it.

☆ ☆ ☆ ☆ ☆ ☆ ☆ ☆ ☆ ☆ ☆ ☆ ☆ ☆ ☆ ☆ ☆ ☆ ☆ ☆ ☆ ☆ ☆ ☆ ☆

## CHOCOLATE GÂTEAU

*Preparation time: 20 minutes*
*Cooking time: 1 hour*
*Quantity: 1 cake*

3 oz (85 g) plain chocolate
3 oz (85 g) butter or
   margarine
2 large eggs
3 oz (85 g) caster sugar
4 oz (115 g) self-raising
   flour or plain flour with
   l teaspoon baking powder

**For the decoration:**
Rich Chocolate Butter Icing
   (see page 98)
chocolate vermicelli

Preheat the oven to 160°C (325°F), Gas Mark 3. Line a 7 inch (18 cm) cake tin with greased greaseproof paper.

Break the chocolate into small pieces, put in a heatproof bowl and melt over a pan of hot water. Cool slightly. Melt the butter or margarine in another bowl. Separate the eggs, add the yolks with the sugar to the chocolate and whisk until thick and creamy. Sift the flour, or flour and baking powder, into the other ingredients then add the melted butter or margarine. Fold the ingredients gently together.

Whisk the egg whites until they stand in soft peaks. Take a tablespoon of the whites and beat briskly into the chocolate mixture then gently fold in the remainder. Spoon into the cake tin and bake for about 1 hour or until firm to a gentle touch. Cool in the tin for 5 minutes then turn out on to a wire rack to cool.

When cold, top with the butter icing and a dusting of chocolate vermicelli.

### VARIATION

Make three times the amount of the Rich Chocolate Butter Icing. Split the cake through the centre and fill with some of the icing. Cover the sides and top of the cake with the remainder of the icing, then coat with chocolate vermicelli.

## LEMON SPONGE

*Preparation time: 20 minutes*
*Cooking time: 30 minutes*
*Quantity: 1 sponge cake*

It may be surprising to anyone who has not used dried eggs to learn they make very good sponges and that the reconstituted eggs whisk up well with the sugar. The sponge is lighter if you can spare an extra 1 oz (25 g) sugar.

This is one of the recipes where cooks were inclined to use the electric whisk for the whole process of making the sponge. While the machine is ideal for whisking the eggs and sugar, it is essential to fold in the flour by hand. If you whisk in the flour with an electric beater you destroy the light texture.

3 oz (85 g) flour
   (see method)
3 reconstituted dried eggs
   (see page 10) or
   fresh eggs
3 oz (85 g) caster sugar
$\frac{1}{2}$–1 teaspoon finely grated
   lemon zest
1 tablespoon lemon juice

**For the filling (optional):**
lemon curd or lemon
   marmalade

**For Lemon Icing:**
6 oz (175 g) icing sugar,
   sifted
little lemon juice

Sift the flour on to a plate and leave at room temperature for at least 30 minutes. This lightens the flour. This sponge can be made with plain flour, without any raising agent, for the lightness incorporated into the eggs and sugar makes the sponge rise. It may be wiser if you have not made this very light sponge before to use self-raising flour or plain flour sifted with ¼ level teaspoon baking powder.

Preheat the oven to 180°C (350°F), Gas Mark 4. Line a 7–7½ inch (18–19 cm) cake tin with greased greaseproof paper or grease and flour it well. Put the reconstituted dried eggs or fresh eggs with the sugar and lemon zest into a bowl. Using a hand or electric whisk, whisk until the mixture is like a thick cream; you should see the trail of the whisk in the mixture. Sift the flour into a bowl. Using a large metal spoon or spatula, not the electric whisk, gently fold the flour, then the lemon juice, into the mixture.

Pour or spoon the mixture into the tin and bake until firm to a gentle touch. Allow to cool in the tin for about 5 minutes then turn out on to a wire rack to cool.

If you would like a filling, split the cake horizontally and spread with the lemon curd or marmalade.

For the Lemon Icing, blend the icing sugar with enough lemon juice to give a firm spreading consistency. Put on to the top of the sponge and spread with a warm knife.

**VARIATION**

Divide the mixture between two 7–7½ inch (18–19 cm) sandwich tins and bake for 12–15 minutes.
**Ginger Icing:** This icing (referred to in Ginger Buns on page 79) is made as the Lemon Icing for Lemon Sponge, above. Blend ¼–½ level teaspoon ground ginger with the icing sugar, or omit the ground ginger and mix the icing sugar with syrup from preserved ginger.

## ATHOLL CAKES

*Preparation time: 20 minutes*
*Cooking time: 12–15 minutes*
*Quantity: 9–12 cakes*

3 oz (85 g) butter or margarine
3 oz (85 g) caster sugar
1½ teaspoons finely grated
   lemon zest
3 oz (85 g) plain flour with
   1 teaspoon baking powder
1 oz (25 g) rice flour or cornflour
1 egg
1½ tablespoons lemon juice
2 tablespoons finely chopped
   candied lemon peel

Grease and flour 9–12 patty tins or put paper cases in the tins. Preheat the oven to 190°C (375°F), Gas Mark 5. Cream the butter or margarine with the sugar and lemon zest. Sift the flour with the baking powder and rice flour or cornflour.

Beat the egg, add to the creamed ingredients with the flour mixture, lemon juice and peel. Spoon into the tins or paper cases and bake the cakes until firm.

## AUSTRALIAN CAKES

*Preparation time: 10 minutes*
*Cooking time: 12 minutes*
*Quantity: 12 cakes*

4 oz (115 g) self-raising flour
   with 1 teaspoon baking
   powder or plain flour with
   2 teaspoons baking powder
4 oz (115 g) cornflakes
3 oz (85 g) butter or margarine
4 oz (115 g) sugar
1 egg
milk, to mix

**For the decoration:**
6 glacé cherries

Preheat the oven to 200°C (400°F), Gas Mark 6. Grease and flour 2 baking trays. Sift the flour and baking powder; lightly crush the cornflakes. Rub the fat into the flour, add the sugar, cornflakes, beaten egg and enough milk to make a sticky consistency.

Put spoonfuls of the mixture on the trays, allowing space for the mixture to spread out. Top each cake with a halved cherry and bake until firm.

## INVALID FARE

I have always found it strange that towards the end of the 1940s and into the early 1950s I was asked to provide recipes for special diets, both at Harrods Food Advice Bureau and on BBC Television. I think everyone was so busy during the war years that minor complaints would be ignored. Now the war was over, there was time to think about aches and pains. The fact that more foods were coming into the country made it possible to prepare the dishes given here.

## BEEF TEA

*Preparation time: 10 minutes*
*Cooking time: 2 hours*
*Quantity: 1 helping, about ¹/₂ pint (300 ml)*

The instruction about using this flavoursome clear soup quickly was very necessary at the time the recipe was written, for the majority of homes still did not contain a refrigerator and freezers were unknown.

8 oz (225 g) lean stewing beef
¹/₂ pint (300 ml) water
pinch salt

Cut the meat into neat dice. Put into a strong jug or the top of a double saucepan. Add the water and salt. Cover the container and stand over a pan of simmering water. Allow the water to simmer steadily for 2 hours then strain the beef tea through muslin.

Leave the beef tea until quite cold then skim any fat from the surface. Heat, adjust the seasoning and serve with crisp toast.

Do not make large quantities of beef tea, for it should not be kept longer than a day.

## HADDOCK QUENELLES

*Preparation time: 15 minutes*
*Cooking time: 10 minutes*
*Quantity: 4 helpings*

People often forget how difficult it was to get good fish during the war years, so many fishermen were at sea in the Royal Navy or the Merchant Navy. The variety of fish was limited and often it was far from fresh when it arrived on the fishmonger's slab. Now numerous pre-war varieties were becoming available again and cooks were returning to some of the well-remembered classic recipes. This fish dish would be ideal for all the family, as well as for an invalid.

10 oz (300 g) haddock fillet, weight when skinned and boned
2 oz (50 g) butter or margarine
2 egg yolks or 1 reconstituted dried egg (see page 10)
4 tablespoons soft breadcrumbs
salt and pepper
1 pint (600 ml) milk

Rub the blade of a sharp knife over the raw fish to get fine flakes. Put these into a basin and pound well to give a smooth texture. Melt the butter or margarine and add to the fish with all the rest of the ingredients, except the milk. Form into 8 finger shapes.

Pour the milk into a large frying pan, add a little seasoning and bring to the boil, then lower the heat so the milk is just simmering.

Poach the quenelles in the milk for 10 minutes. Turn them around several times so they cook evenly. Lift the fish on to a heated dish, and keep warm while making a sauce with the milk.

### VARIATIONS

Use whiting instead of haddock. Finely chopped parsley or a little dried parsley can be added to the fish.

**Chicken Quenelles:** Substitute minced raw chicken breast for the fish. Poach for 15 minutes.

### CHICKEN TERRAPIN

*Preparation time: 10 minutes*
*Cooking time: 12 minutes*
*Quantity: 1 helping*

1 egg
½ oz (15 g) butter
  or margarine
2 teaspoons flour
4 tablespoons milk
salt and pepper
1 oz (25 g) cooked rice
2 oz (50 g) cooked chicken
  breast
few drops lemon juice

**To garnish:**

toast triangles

Hard-boil the egg, and cool it quickly in cold water. Shell and chop the egg. Heat the butter or margarine, stir in the flour and the milk and continue stirring to make a thick sauce. Add the chopped egg and the rest of the ingredients and heat thoroughly. Form into a neat round on a heated plate and garnish with triangles of crisp toast.

### BACON AND CHICKEN TOAST

*Preparation time: 10 minutes*
*Cooking time: 8 minutes*
*Quantity: 1 helping*

1 lean bacon rasher, derinded
1 oz (25 g) butter or margarine
1 egg
3 tablespoons finely diced
  cooked chicken
salt and pepper
1 slice bread

Cut the bacon rasher into small pieces. Cook in a pan until crisp. Meanwhile, place half the butter or margarine in a basin. Stand over a pan of boiling water. Add the beaten egg, chicken and seasoning and stir until the egg is just set. Toast the bread, spread with the remaining butter or margarine. Top with the bacon, then the egg and chicken mixture.

### PLAICE AND TOMATO FILLETS

*Preparation time:*
*10 minutes*
*Cooking time: 10 minutes*
*Quantity: 1–2 helpings*

1 medium tomato,
  skinned and halved
2 small plaice fillets,
  skinned
1 oz (25 g) butter
  or margarine
salt and pepper
2 tablespoons milk

Place half a tomato on each fish fillet, roll round the tomato and put on to a plate. Top with the butter or margarine, add a little seasoning and the milk. Cover with a second plate and place over boiling water. Steam the fish for 10 minutes.

The small amount of liquid makes an unthickened sauce.

**VARIATION**

Use tomato juice instead of milk.

## SAVOURY EGG

*Preparation time: 5 minutes*
*Cooking time: 5 minutes*
*Quantity: 1 helping*

1 oz (25 g) butter or margarine
2 tablespoons milk
1 teaspoon Worcestershire sauce
1 teaspoon finely chopped
    parsley
1 teaspoon finely chopped
    spring onion
salt and pepper
1 egg
1 slice bread

Put half the butter or margarine with the milk, sauce, parsley, onion and a very little seasoning into a small pan. Bring just to boiling point.

Break the egg into a cup and carefully slide into the hot liquid. Poach gently, spooning the savoury liquid over the egg until the white is just set.

Toast the bread, spread with the remaining butter or margarine and top with the egg. Serve at once.

## LEMON BARLEY WATER

*Preparation time: 10 minutes*
*Cooking time: 3 minutes*
*Quantity: nearly 1³/₄ pints (1 litre)*

As both lemons and pearl barley were now obtainable, this refreshing drink formed part of one invalid menu I demonstrated on television.

    3 oz (85 g) pearl barley
    2 lemons
    1½ pints (900 ml) water
    2 oz (50 g) sugar, or to taste

Put the pearl barley into a saucepan and cover with cold water. Bring to the boil and allow to boil for 3 minutes. Strain the barley and discard the water. This blanching process whitens the barley and gives it a better texture and taste. Tip the barley into a large jug.

Pare the zest from the lemons and put into a saucepan with the 1½ pints (900 ml) water. Bring the water to the boil and pour over the barley. Add the sugar. Leave until cold, then strain and add the lemon juice.

## EGG IN POTATO CREAM

*Preparation time: 10 minutes*
*Cooking time: 10–15 minutes*
*Quantity: 1 helping*

Cream was not available for several years after the war ended so we still had to be content with the top of the milk. In spite of this, we tended to use the term 'cream' in many recipes.

    4 oz (115 g) cooked potatoes
    1 oz (25 g) butter or margarine
    1 tablespoon cream (from top
        of the milk)
    2 tablespoons grated cheese
    salt and pepper
    1 egg

If the potatoes are leftover, heat them gently in a saucepan, mash well then add half the butter or margarine, the cream, half the grated cheese and a little seasoning. Form into a ring shape on an ovenproof plate. Break the egg into the centre of the ring and top this with the last of the cheese and fat. Preheat the oven to 200°C (400°F), Gas Mark 6 and bake for 10–15 minutes. Serve at once.

**Whatever the pleasure
Player's complete it**

*Player's Please*

PLAYER'S NAVY CUT CIGARETTES & TOBACCO          [NCC 784K]

*It's worth going .*          *out of your . . .*

*way to get . .*          *SILMOS LOLLIES!*

## MILK JELLY

When jelly tablets became more plentiful and of a better quality many recipes were devised using them. I remember demonstrating how to make individual portions of a milk jelly — ideal for an invalid — as part of a television programme on dishes for the invalid. I presented a tray showing several dishes suitable for someone not well in front of the cameras, quite ignoring the heat of the studio, which was much hotter then than in modern times. While I spoke about the dishes there was a sudden gurgle and the milk jelly collapsed into a pool of liquid — so much for an attractive invalid tray!

To make a milk jelly that does not curdle, simply dissolve the jelly tablet in ¼ pint (150 ml) very hot water. Allow to cool, but not set, then make up to 1 pint (568 ml — not 600 ml, in this case) with cold milk. Pour into a large mould or several small moulds and leave until set.

# ★1953★

THIS WAS A **year of great celebrations in honour of the Coronation of Queen Elizabeth II on 2 June. This Coronation was unique in that people throughout Britain, and in other countries too, who owned television sets could watch the solemn and moving ceremony and share the excitement of the cheering crowds who lined the route to Westminster Abbey. Open house was offered to many neighbours and friends so they could share in the rejoicing on this splendid occasion, with all the best of British pageantry.**

Queen Elizabeth and Prince Philip came out on to the balcony of Buckingham Palace six times during the evening to acknowledge the cheers of the crowd. There was a firework display on the Victoria Embankment of the Thames in London.

A British expedition had been attempting to climb to the top of Mount Everest. On 1 June, to add to the feeling of national pride, it was announced that the summit had been reached by the New Zealander, Edmund Hillary, with Sherpa Tenzing Norgay. British heads were certainly held high during June of 1953.

Earlier in the year there had been bad news. In February, the east coast of England had been devasted by floods, caused by hurricane winds and exceptionally high tides. Sea defences collapsed from Lincolnshire to Kent. Early reports were that over 280 people had lost their lives, many people were missing and thousands were made homeless. There were dramatic rescues of people trapped on the roofs of their houses. The total damage was estimated at hundreds of millions of pounds.

Queen Mary, the widow of George V and grandmother of the present Queen, died in her sleep in March, aged 86. This dignified lady had not changed her style of dress for 50 years. She wore long dresses and coats and elaborate toques and carried a gold-topped cane.

In spite of the peace talks signed in 1952, fighting had continued in South Korea. In July, it was announced that at last the guns would fall silent. About two million men and women been killed in this war.

In December, smog (fog) masks were made available on the National Health Service for the sum of one shilling (5 p). These were to counteract the effect of the bad fogs (known as pea-soupers) in industrial areas of Britain.

In March, eggs came off ration. This was most welcome, for people had missed eggs almost more than other foods. Dried eggs had been a valuable stop-gap, although there were two different opinions about them. Some people loved them, others were ultra-critical of their flavour. With greater supplies, the freshness of eggs improved a great deal.

In April, real cream became available once more. This was never rationed for it was illegal for dairy farmers to produce cream for sale. It is strange to think that many younger teenagers had never tasted cream. Reaction about cream was mixed; older people greeted it with enthusiasm, younger people with some reservations, since many found it rich and greasy and declared they preferred evaporated milk.

In September, sugar was taken off ration. This was a good season to have more supplies of sugar, for bottling fruit in syrup, rather than water, and making plum and other jams.

## CORONATION DAY

2 June 1953 was celebrated throughout Britain and the Commonwealth for television helped people everywhere feel they were very much part of the event. There was this feeling that we were entering into a new and exciting second Elizabethan era and that the young queen headed a nation that might well reflect the glories of her illustrious predecessor.

At this time, only a minority of homes had television so most people who owned a set kept 'open house' so they shared the excitement with friends and neighbours. Party food was the order of the day and the recipes in this section were typical of those made for the celebrations. Fortunately, this year saw the end of some rationing so catering was easier and more enjoyable. The meal at lunchtime was generally in the form of a buffet.

## SALMON DIP

Dips were relatively new at this time. This was a good dish to serve with drinks on Coronation Day. The French term 'crudités', meaning raw vegetables, was gradually becoming known. This dip is sufficient for 6.

Flake 8 oz (225 g) well-drained cooked or canned salmon (weight without skin and bones) and mix with 1 tablespoon lemon juice, 5 tablespoons mayonnaise, 2 tablespoons double cream, 1 tablespoon tomato ketchup, 3 tablespoons finely grated cucumber (without skin) and 2 teaspoons chopped parsley or fennel leaves with seasoning to taste.

Put into a small bowl on a large platter and surround with narrow strips of raw carrots, red and green peppers, radishes and crisp small biscuits to dip into the creamy mixture.

## CORONATION CHICKEN

*Preparation time: 25 minutes*
*Cooking time: 1¼ hours*
*Quantity: 6–8 helpings*

This recipe has been known since the Coronation as the dish of the day. There have been several versions, but basically it is a mixture of cold chicken, fruit and a mild curry-flavoured dressing. Curry paste was less well-known than curry powder in 1953; it is better for cold dishes but curry powder could be substituted. Real cream was available by the time of the Coronation. The chicken can be roasted but it is much more moist if steamed or, better still, simmered in water with an onion, several carrots and herbs.

### For cooking the chicken:
1 chicken, about 4 lb (1.8 kg) when trussed
1 onion, sliced
2–3 carrots, sliced
small sprig parsley
small sprig tarragon
salt and pepper

### For the salad:
10–12 oz (300–350 g) can halved apricots
7½ fl oz (225 ml) mayonnaise
2 teaspoons curry paste, or to taste
4 tablespoons single cream
2 tablespoons fruit syrup
3 oz (85 g) blanched flaked almonds
mixed salad ingredients (see method)

Put the chicken into a large saucepan with the other ingredients for cooking. Cover and simmer gently until just tender. When cold, skin the chicken, take the meat off the bones and cut it into bite-sized pieces.

Drain the apricots and cut into thin slices, saving 2 tablespoons of the syrup (the rest can be used in a fruit salad). Mix the mayonnaise with the curry paste, cream and fruit syrup. Add the chicken, apricots and half the nuts. Pile neatly on to a dish; top with the remaining nuts. Serve in a border of finely shredded lettuce, thin slices of tomato and cucumber.

### VARIATIONS
Add chopped spring onions to give a more savoury taste.
Use fresh or canned pineapple instead of apricots.

## HUZARENSIA

*Preparation: 25 minutes*
*No cooking*
*Quantity: 4 helpings*

This Hussar's Salad, with its beef meat content, became a great favourite.

6 oz (175 g) cooked tender beef, neatly diced
1 lb (450 g) cooked new potatoes, neatly diced
2 small cooked beetroot, peeled and diced
1 large cooking apple, peeled and diced
2–3 tablespoons small cocktail pickled onions
2–3 tablespoons diced pickled gherkins

**For the dressing:**
1–2 teaspoons French mustard
3 tablespoons mayonnaise
1 teaspoon vinegar from pickles

**To garnish:**
mixed salad

Mix all the ingredients together then blend with the dressing and arrange in the centre of the mixed salad.

## LINZERTORTE

*Preparation time: 30 minutes*
*Cooking time: 30–35 minutes*
*Quantity: 6–8 helpings*

This Austrian spiced tart could only be made when ground almonds became available.

**For the pastry:**
6 oz (175 g) butter or margarine
2 oz (50 g) caster sugar
1 teaspoon finely grated lemon zest
1 egg
8 oz (225 g) plain flour
$\frac{1}{2}$ teaspoon ground cinnamon
2 oz (50 g) ground almonds

**For the topping:**
1 lb (450 g) fresh raspberries
sugar to taste
2 tablespoons redcurrant jelly
1 tablespoon water
little icing sugar

For the pastry, cream the butter or margarine and sugar with the lemon zest. Add the beaten egg, then then fold in the flour, cinnamon and almonds. Turn out on to a lightly floured board and knead until smooth. Wrap and chill for at least 30 minutes.

Roll out two-thirds of the dough into a round to fit inside an 8 inch (20 cm) fluted flan ring placed on an upturned baking tray (this makes it easy to slide off when cooked). Roll out the remaining pastry into narrow strips $\frac{1}{4}$ inch (6 mm) thick and 8½ inches (21 cm) long. Put the raspberries over the base, dust with a little sugar then cover with a lattice of the strips. Moisten the ends and seal well.

Preheat the oven to 180°C (350°F), Gas Mark 4 and bake for 30–35 minutes or until firm. Allow the tart to become cold.

Melt the jelly with the water then brush over the fruit. Dust with sifted icing sugar.

SURELY LARD IS FINE FOR PASTRY!

...AND SO IS MARGE!

but...Spry makes Pastry Lighter

## CHICKEN AND MUSHROOM SALAD

*Preparation time: 15 minutes*
*Cooking time: 3–4 minutes*
*for the mushrooms*
*Quantity: 4 helpings*

8 oz (225 g) cooked chicken, diced
4 oz (115 g) celery heart, diced
2 tablespoons sliced or chopped olives
little mayonnaise
lettuce
watercress
1 oz (25 g) butter or margarine
4 oz (115 g) button mushrooms

Mix the chicken, celery and olives with mayonnaise. Spoon on to a bed of lettuce and watercress.

Melt the butter or margarine and lightly fry the button mushrooms. Spoon on to the salad immediately before serving.

## END OF SWEET RATIONING

February 1953 saw the end of sweet rationing — a joy for
the children and for many adults, too. I was 'deluged' with requests
for real chocolate icings to put on cakes — often bought from the
baker — and for chocolate cakes and desserts.

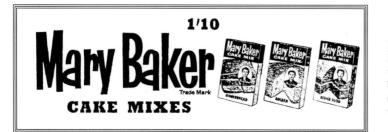

### RICH CHOCOLATE BUTTER ICING

Melt 2 oz (50 g) plain or milk chocolate in a heatproof bowl over hot
water. Cool slightly. Add 1 oz (25 g)
butter and beat well then sift in 2 oz
(50 g) icing sugar and 2 or 3 drops
vanilla essence.

**GROWING UP
ON THE COCOA HABIT**

## CHOCOLATE BISCUITS

*Preparation time: 15 minutes
Cooking time: 15 minutes
Quantity: 24–30 biscuits*

4 oz (115 g) margarine
4 oz (115 g) caster sugar
few drops vanilla essence
2 oz (50 g) plain flour
1 oz (25 g) rice flour or
 cornflour
2 oz (50 g) chocolate powder

**For the Chocolate Icing:**
3 oz (85 g) plain or milk
 chocolate
½ oz (15 g) butter

Preheat the oven to 160°C (325°F), Gas Mark 3. Lightly grease two baking trays.

Cream the margarine, sugar and vanilla until light. Sift the flour with the rice flour or cornflour and chocolate powder. Add to the creamed ingredients and knead well. If the mixture seems a little sticky, wrap and chill for a time.

Roll out the dough to ¼ inch (6 mm) thick and cut into rounds or fancy shapes. Put on to the prepared trays and prick lightly. Bake for 15 minutes, or until firm. Cool on the trays.

Break the chocolate for the Chocolate Icing into small pieces and put into a heatproof bowl with the butter. Melt over a pan of hot water – do not leave too long or the chocolate will lose its gloss. Cool slightly, then spread over the biscuits with a flat-bladed knife.

## UNCOOKED CHOCOLATE CAKE

*Preparation time: 20 minutes
No cooking
Quantity: 1 cake*

8 oz (225 g) plain sweet or
 digestive biscuits
3 oz (85 g) plain chocolate
3 oz (85 g) butter or margarine
1 oz (25 g) caster sugar
few drops vanilla essence
1 level tablespoon golden syrup

**For the topping:**
2 oz (50 g) butter or margarine
few drops vanilla essence
4 oz (115 g) icing sugar
approximately 2 teaspoons
 milk
1–2 oz (25–50 g) chocolate drops

Crush the biscuits into fine crumbs. Break the chocolate into small pieces, put in a heatproof bowl and melt over hot water. Cool slightly. Add the butter or margarine with the sugar, vanilla and syrup to the chocolate and beat until soft and creamy. Add the crumbs and mix well.

Place a 7–8 inch (18–20 cm) flan ring on a serving plate and fill with the crumb mixture. Press down very firmly and chill overnight or for several hours. Remove the flan ring.

Cream the butter or margarine for the topping with the vanilla, sift in the icing sugar and mix well. Gradually beat in enough milk to give a fairly firm spreading consistency. Coat the top of the cake then decorate with the chocolate drops.

## CHOCOLATE FLOATING ISLANDS

*Preparation time: 20 minutes
Cooking time: 20 minutes
Quantity: 4 helpings*

As well as being able to use chocolate in cooking, there were more fresh eggs available and one could make meringues and meringue toppings for desserts.

In this version of the classic dish, the egg whites are poached in water so they remain white. The custard mixture, made with chocolate and egg yolks, is partially thickened with a little cornflour, which helps to prevent the egg mixture curdling.

3 oz (85 g) plain chocolate
1 pint (600 ml) milk
1 teaspoon cornflour
3 large eggs
4 oz (115 g) caster sugar
½ teaspoon vanilla essence

**For the decoration:**
1 oz (25 g) plain
 chocolate

Break the chocolate into pieces. Pour ¾ pint (450 ml) of the milk into a saucepan, add the chocolate and heat until it has melted. Blend the cornflour with the remaining cold milk. Separate the eggs, add the yolks and half the sugar to the cornflour mixture and beat well. Pour into the chocolate-flavoured milk.

Either leave the mixture in the saucepan or transfer it to a basin placed over a pan of hot water. Cook slowly, whisking most of the time, until the custard thickens sufficiently to coat the back of a wooden spoon. Pour into a serving dish, cover and leave until cold.

Meanwhile, whisk the egg whites until very stiff. Gradually beat in the remaining sugar. Pour about 1 pint (600 ml) water into a frying pan, and add the vanilla essence. Bring just to boiling point then lower the heat so the water simmers steadily. Drop spoonfuls of the meringue on to the water. Poach for 2 minutes then carefully turn over and poach on the second side. Lift on to a sieve placed over a plate and leave until cold. Spoon on to the chocolate mixture.

Grate the chocolate for the decoration over the meringues. Serve very cold.

## LEMON MERINGUE PIE

*Preparation time: 30 minutes*
*Cooking time: 50 minutes*
*Quantity: 4–6 helpings*

I can still remember my feeling of pleasure when I was able to demonstrate a real Lemon Meringue Pie on BBC Television.

**For the short or sweet shortcrust pastry:**
6 oz (175 g) flour etc. (see Gypsy Tart, page 21, or Oriental Fingers, page 67)

**For the filling:**
2 small or 1 large lemon(s)
1 oz (25 g) cornflour or custard powder, whichever is available
approx. ½ pint (300 ml) water (see method)
2 oz (50 g) caster sugar
2 egg yolks
½–1 oz (15–25 g) butter or margarine

**For the meringue:**
2 egg whites
2–4 oz (50–115 g) caster sugar (see method)

Make the pastry as on page 21 or 67. Preheat the oven to 200°C (400°F), Gas Mark 6 if using shortcrust pastry, but only to 190°C (375°F), Gas Mark 5 if using sweet shortcrust pastry. Roll out the pastry and use to line a 7–8 inch (18–20 cm) flan tin or ring on an upturned baking tray. Bake blind (see page 47) for 15 minutes or until the pastry is firm but still pale in colour. Remove the pastry shell from the oven and reduce the oven temperature to 150°C (300°F), Gas Mark 2.

While the pastry is cooking prepare the filling. Grate the lemon(s) finely to give 1–1½ teaspoons lemon zest. Use just the coloured part of the rind so there is no bitter pith. Halve the lemon(s) and squeeze out the juice. You need 3 tablespoons, or 4 tablespoons if you like a very sharp flavour.

Blend the cornflour or custard powder with the cold water. Use the full quantity with 3 tablespoons lemon juice but remove 1 tablespoon water if using the larger amount of fruit juice. Pour into a saucepan, add the lemon zest and juice. Stir over a low heat until the mixture has thickened well. Remove from the heat. Whisk the egg yolks and stir into the lemon mixture with the butter or margarine. Spoon into the partially cooked pastry case, return to the oven and bake for 10 minutes.

For the meringue, whisk the egg whites until stiff and gradually fold in the amount of sugar required. If serving the pie hot, you can use the smaller amount. Spoon over the lemon filling and bake for 25 minutes.

## CHEESE AND HADDOCK SOUFFLÉ

As the war had put an end to formal long menus in the majority of homes, soufflés had come to be regarded more as light main dishes or an hors d'oeuvre for a three-course meal rather than as a savoury at the end of a meal.

This dish became quite famous when reports circulated that it was a favourite with the Duke and Duchess of Windsor.

*Preparation time: 15 minutes*
*Cooking time: 15 or 25–30 minutes (see method)*
*Quantity: 4–6 helpings, as hors d'oeuvre*

1 oz (25 g) butter or margarine
1 oz (25 g) flour
¼ pint (150 ml) milk
3 tablespoons single cream or top of the milk
½ teaspoon finely grated lemon zest
1 teaspoon lemon juice
3 eggs
2 oz (50 g) Parmesan cheese, grated
3 oz (85 g) smoked haddock, finely flaked
salt and pepper
1 egg white

Preheat the oven to 190°C (375°F), Gas Mark 5. Grease one 6 inch (15 cm) soufflé dish or 4–6 individual soufflé dishes.

Heat the butter or margarine in a large saucepan, stir in the flour then add the milk and cream. Bring to the boil and stir briskly as it becomes a thick sauce. Remove from the heat and stir in the lemon zest and juice.

Separate the eggs and beat the yolks into the sauce, then the cheese and haddock. Do not reheat. Taste the mixture and season.

Whisk the 4 egg whites until quite stiff, then gently fold them into the other ingredients. Spoon into the dish or dishes. Bake the small soufflés for approximately 1 5 minutes or the large one for 25–30 minutes. The soufflé is nicer if well risen and golden brown but still slightly soft in the centre. Serve at once.

**VARIATION**
Use finely grated mature Cheddar cheese instead of Parmesan.

Oh joy! real cream today-and every day
*(And so wonderfully cheap too)*

## EGGS OFF RATION

Although most people had become very accustomed to
using dried eggs in all kinds of recipes from omelettes to
batters and cakes, it was a great joy to have shell eggs
off ration. Immediately, I was asked about making
meringues and meringue toppings for desserts, such as the
popular Lemon Meringue Pie, which I have included here.
Although dried eggs made an acceptable soufflé, the result
with fresh eggs, where the yolks and whites could be
separated, was infinitely better.

# ★1954★

**I**N FEBRUARY OF **this year Queen Elizabeth with Prince Philip arrived in Australia for their tour. This was the first time a reigning monarch had visited the country.** *Gothic,* **the ship in which they arrived, was greeted by about 500 craft and crowds of cheering people. Their children, Prince Charles and Princess Anne, stayed in Britain, in the charge of their grandmother, Queen Elizabeth the Queen Mother.**

The scope of television was clearly illustrated in June when Pope Pius XII appeared on British television screens simultaneously with his appearance on the screens of seven other European nations.

I was the subject of an interesting incident this year. One afternoon I had been demonstrating how to make bread on BBC Television. When I arrived home I was asked to telephone the BBC, who told me with great excitement that they had received a call from America during the course of the transmission saying 'they could see a dame making a pud'. The reception was entirely due to freak weather conditions, not to satellites, so I was the first person ever to be received on American television direct from Britain.

One piece of news that was received very seriously by many people was that the plague myxomatosis was affecting rabbits even more seriously than it had done in 1953. In some places, Kent in particular, the rabbit population was almost entirely wiped out. For the past years rabbits had helped to eke out the meat ration.

For several years, there had been much talk about runners achieving a four-minute mile.

This was the year it happened! Roger Bannister, a medical student, achieved the distance in 3 minutes 59.4 seconds.

In June of this year Winston Churchill and the American President Eisenhower signed the Potomac Agreement in Washington. The President was famous for his leadership during the war. The Agreement emphasised the comradeship of the two countries and their pursuit of world peace and justice.

In May all fats, such as butter, margarine and cooking fat, came off ration. This gave rise to advertising campaigns on the rival merits of individual fats for various cooking purposes.

In June meat was finally removed from rationing. This was the last of all rationed foods to be derestricted. Throughout the years from 1940 lack of meat had caused great problems to the population. We were a nation of meat-eaters who longed for juicy steaks and roasts. At last these would be coming. The major meat market at Smithfield, London, normally opened for business in the morning at 6 a.m. In celebration of meat being freed from rationing it opened six hours early, at midnight, so supplies could be sent out early to butchers in anticipation of a great rush of customers.

Ration books were no longer necessary and many people burned theirs or ripped them up in anticipation of easier times ahead.

Nutritionists of the future would say we were a healthier nation during the long years of rationing. The British people were not thinking of that in 1954. They were just so thankful that they could shop at leisure, avoid queues for various foods and buy the ingredients that they and their families liked best.

## FATS OFF RATIONING

The derationing of all fats made a great difference to the kind of cooking done. I was deluged with requests to demonstrate flaky and puff pastry. Often I had a frantic telephone call at Harrods from someone making puff pastry to say 'it has become sticky (or greasy); what do I do?'

It was quite difficult to make people, who had never made these richer pastries before the war, to realise you had to be patient and allow the pastry to rest in a cool place — obviously, the refrigerator (if you had one) — between foldings and rollings.

Frying became a popular form of cooking, for fat was not regarded as the health hazard it is today. When discussing food values in 1954, it was accepted that fats created warmth in the body and were an excellent source of energy.

## MAKING CHIPS

The only way most people could produce fried potatoes before the ending of fat rationing was by shallow frying in the little amount of fat they had saved or to use the oven method, which was not real frying but a very acceptable substitute. You greased and heated a flat baking tray, laid potato slices (chips were the wrong shape for this method) in a single layer on the hot tray, brushed them with a few drops of melted fat and cooked them at a high temperature. In 1954, electric deep-fat fryers were not used and oil was used only rarely for cooking, so frying chips would be done in an ordinary pan with a frying basket (if you had one), with lard or cooking fat as the frying medium.

**To make the chips:** Peel potatoes, cut into finger shapes, and keep in cold water until required then dry very well before cooking.

**To cook the chips:** Put lard or cooking fat (or oil if you prefer) into the pan, which must never be more than half full. Heat to 170°C (340°F). To test without a thermometer, drop a cube of day-old bread into the hot fat. It should turn golden coloured in one minute. If it changes colour in a shorter time than this, then the fat is too hot and must be allowed to cool slightly.

Put in the potatoes (if you have a large number, fry them in batches) and cook steadily for 6–7 minutes, or until tender but still pale. Remove on to a dish.

Just before serving, reheat the fat or oil until it reaches 190°C (375°F) – a cube of day-old bread should turn golden within 30 seconds. Fry the potatoes for a second time until they are crisp and golden brown.

Turn out the potatoes on to absorbent paper to drain then serve. The potatoes can be sprinkled with a little salt before serving. Garnish with parsley.

## LOBSTER CUTLETS

*Preparation time: 20 minutes*
*Cooking time: 8 minutes, plus 25 minutes for the sauce etc.*
*Quantity: 4 helpings*

**For the cutlets:**
1 medium-sized cooked
   lobster
1 oz (25 g) butter or
   margarine
1 oz (25 g) flour
¼ pint (150 ml) milk
½ teaspoon finely grated
   lemon zest
1 tablespoon finely grated
   onion
1 egg
salt and pepper
4 oz (115 g) soft fine
   breadcrumbs
2 teaspoons chopped parsley

**For coating and frying:**
1 tablespoon flour
1 egg
2 oz (50 g) fine crisp
   breadcrumbs
2 oz (50 g) fat

**For the sauce:**
2 oz (50 g) butter or
   margarine
2 oz (50 g) mushrooms,
   finely chopped
1 tablespoon finely chopped
   onion
1 oz (25 g) flour
¼ pint (150 ml) lobster stock
   (see method)
¼ pint (150 ml) milk
3 tablespoons cream or
   top of the milk
few drops Worcestershire
   sauce

Remove the shell from the lobster and place the shell in a pan with water to cover. Put a lid on the pan and simmer for 8 minutes, then strain. This gives stock with the flavour required for the sauce. Remove the intestinal vein from the lobster and finely dice the flesh.

Melt the butter or margarine for the cutlets, stir in the flour and then the milk, lemon zest and onion. Stir briskly as the sauce comes to the boil and becomes very thick. Add the lobster and the rest of the ingredients for the cutlets. Mix well then chill for a time. Form into 4 large or 8 small cutlet shapes.

Coat in the flour, then in the beaten egg and crumbs. Heat the fat and fry the cutlets until crisp and brown on both sides.

Melt the butter or margarine for the sauce, add the mushrooms and onion, cook gently for 5 minutes then blend in the flour, the lobster stock and milk. Stir briskly as the sauce comes to the boil and thickens, add the cream, Worcestershire sauce and seasoning.

Serve the lobster cutlets with the sauce, garnishing the dish with the very small lobster claws, if liked.

## PUFF PASTRY

When fat came off the ration it gave people a wonderful opportunity to make richer cakes and pastries. I demonstrated making flaky and puff pastry with great regularity at Harrods Food Advice Bureau.

   8 oz (225 g) plain flour
   pinch salt
   squeeze lemon juice
   water, to bind
   8 oz (225 g) butter

Sift the flour and salt into a mixing bowl. Add the lemon juice and enough cold water to make a pliable dough.
**Stage 1.** Roll out to a neat oblong (see sketch on page 106) and place the butter in the centre.
**Stage 2.** Fold the corners A and B over the pastry, hinging at C and D, to cover the butter. Bring down the top third of the dough, E to C and F to D.
**Stage 3.** Turn the dough at right angles so you have the open end towards you.
**Stage 4.** Depress the dough at intervals (known as ribbing the pastry).
**Stage 5.** Roll out the dough to an oblong. Fold as Stage 2 then repeat Stages 3 and 4. Continue like this, giving 7 rollings and 7 foldings in all.

### A MODERN TOUCH
Strong (bread-making) flour is excellent for this pastry and for Flaky Pastry.

## FLAKY PASTRY

8 oz (225 g) plain flour
pinch salt
6 oz (175 g) butter, or half
    butter or best margarine
    and half lard
squeeze lemon juice
water to bind

Sift the flour and salt into a mixing bowl. Divide the fat into three portions and cut into small dice. Rub one third of the fat into the flour, then add the lemon juice and sufficient water to give a pliable dough.

**Stage 1.** Roll out the dough to an oblong shape.

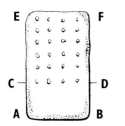

**Stage 2.** Dot the second third of the fat over the top two-thirds of the dough, as shown in the sketch.

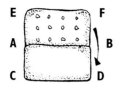

**Stage 3.** Fold the corners A and B over the pastry, hinging at C and D, to cover the fat. Bring down the top third of the dough, E to C and F to D.

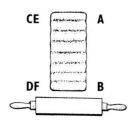

**Stage 4.** Turn the dough at right angles so you have the open end towards you. Continue rolling and folding so you do 3 rollings and foldings.

## VOL-AU-VENTS

These light pastry cases became the most popular pastry dish when people were able to make puff pastry. The days of frozen puff pastry were some little way ahead. Savoury vol-au-vents would be filled with diced fish or meat in a creamy sauce; sweet cases were filled with jam and whipped cream.

Make the Puff Pastry (see page 105) and ensure it is well-chilled before trying to cut out the shapes.

Roll out the dough to ¹/₂–³/₄ inch (1.5–2 cm) thick. Cut into rounds – the size depends upon how large you want the vol-au-vents to be; for medium-sized cases, use a cutter of about 2¹/₂ inches (6.5 cm) in diameter.

Take a 1¹/₂ inch (3.5 cm) cutter and press into the pastry, going approximately half way through the dough. Place on a lightly dampened baking tray. Chill well before baking.

If making the cases for a savoury dish, brush the rims with beaten egg yolk. For a sweet dish, brush with lightly whisked egg white and dust with a very little sugar.

### TO BAKE VOL-AU-VENTS

Preheat the oven to 230°C (450°F), Gas Mark 8. Bake the cases for 10 minutes at this temperature or until they have risen well, then reduce the oven temperature to 180°C (350°F), Gas Mark 4 and continue cooking for a further 5 minutes or until firm.

Carefully remove the centre rounds with a knife, and set them aside to be the lids of the cases after they are filled. If there is any slightly uncooked pastry in the centre, return the cases to the oven and cook for a further few minutes.

If serving hot, fill the hot pastry with the hot filling.

If serving cold, make sure both pastry and filling are cold before putting them together.

## SAUSAGE ROLLS

*Preparation time: 30 minutes*
*Cooking time: 20–25 minutes*
*Quantity: 12 rolls*

Butchers were able to make far better sausages, so the combination of these plus home-made pastry ensured a good result.

Flaky Pastry, made with 6 oz
    (175 g) flour etc. (see left)
8 oz (225 g) sausagemeat

**To glaze:**
1 egg

Preheat the oven to 220°C (425°F), Gas Mark 7. Roll out the pastry until very thin and cut into two long strips, each measuring approximately 5 inches (13 cm) wide. Moisten the edges with water.

Make the sausagemeat into similar lengths and place on the dough. Fold the pastry to enclose the sausagemeat. Press the edges together and flake them by cutting the edges horizontally with a sharp knife to give several layers.

Cut each strip into about 6 portions. Place on a baking tray. Make 2 or 3 slits on top of each roll and brush with the beaten egg. Cook until golden brown and firm. If necessary, lower the oven heat slightly towards the end of the cooking time so that the pastry does not over-brown.

## COMMONWEALTH TOUR

In February 1952 Princess ELizabeth and her husband, Prince Philip, left Britain for a special tour. The Princess was deputising for her father, who was too unwell to travel.

Within a few days the couple had to return from their first stop in Africa as King George VI had died very suddenly.

With the Coronation celebrations in Britain in 1953 it was not until the early days of 1954 that the tour could be rearranged. As one might expect, all the various nations wanted to welcome their new ruler. Queen Elizabeth and her husband visited many of the countries that formed part of the Commonwealth and in each of these they were received with great enthusiasm.

As the picture above shows there were many ceremonial occasions but there was also time to meet people in the various countries and enjoy the different scenery and cultures, plus the warmer weather, which made a contrast to the winter chill of Britain.

## MEAT OFF RATION

When meat came off ration in June 1954 this had a special significance. It meant the end of the rationing of all foods, which had begun in 1940. Ration Books could now be discarded.

Most people had longed for juicy steaks and joints when the supply of meat was so scarce, so to celebrate the end of meat rationing it was certain that cooks would celebrate by buying these. Two of the meat recipes of the time I give here are for ways of serving steak — these were well-known at the time, and now could form part of family fare. There is also a recipe from Czechoslovakia, which symbolizes the increasing interest in dishes from abroad.

## STEAK DIANE

*Preparation time: 10 minutes*
*Cooking time: 4 minutes*
*Quantity: 4 helpings*

2–3 oz (50–85 g) butter
1 onion or shallot, finely chopped
4 very thin slices sirloin or rump steak
1–2 teaspoons Worcestershire sauce, or to taste
few drops brandy (optional)
1 tablespoon chopped parsley

Heat the butter in a large frying pan, add the onion and cook gently for 2 minutes. Add the steaks and cook for 1 minute on either side. Lift out of the pan on to a hot dish. Add the sauce and brandy. Ignite, if wished, add the parsley, then spoon over the steaks.

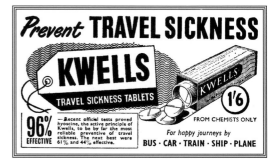

## STEAK AU POIVRE

*Preparation time: 10 minutes*
*Cooking time: 5 minutes, or to taste*
*Quantity: 4 helpings*

1 oz (25 g) peppercorns
3 oz (85 g) butter
4 fillet or rump steaks
3 tablespoons brandy
  (see method)
4 tablespoons beef stock
  (see method)

Lightly crush the peppercorns, press into both sides of the steaks and leave for 20 minutes so the meat absorbs the flavour of the peppercorns. Heat the butter in a large frying pan and cook the steaks to personal taste.

Lift on to a heated dish. Pour the brandy or stock, or use half brandy and half stock, into the pan. Ignite, if wished, then pour over the steaks. Serve with fried potatoes and other vegetables.

## ZNOJEMSKY GULAS

*Preparation time: 25 minutes*
*Cooking time: 45 minutes*
*Quantity: 4 helpings*

This Czech version of Gulasch was given me by a refugee. It is quickly cooked for tender cuts of steak, not stewing beef, are used.

1 lb (450 g) rump or
  sirloin steak
1 oz (25 g) flour
salt and pepper
pinch cayenne pepper
3 oz (85 g) butter or
  margarine
3 medium onions, finely
  chopped
1 tablespoon paprika,
  or to taste
1 pint (600 ml) beef stock
2 tablespoons tomato purée
2 medium potatoes, cut into
  small dice

Cut the meat into 1 inch (2.5 cm) dice. Blend the flour with the seasonings and coat the meat.

Melt the butter or margarine in a large pan, add the meat and fry steadily for 5 minutes. Remove the meat from the pan, then add the onions and cook for 5 minutes. Stir in the paprika, then gradually add the stock. Bring to the boil, add the tomato purée then the potatoes. Cover the pan and simmer for 20 minutes or until the potatoes are softened. Sieve or liquidize the mixture to give a smooth thickened sauce. Return to the pan and add the beef. Cook for 10–15 minutes or to personal taste.

Serve the Gulas with pickled cucumbers or gherkins.

# INDEX

# ACKNOWLEDGEMENTS

Marguerite Patten would like to thank Dr Louise Davies, PhD., F.I.H.Ec. who kindly loaned her copies of *Food and Nutrition*.
Dr Davies created and subsequently edited for the Ministry of Food Booklets which were sent to educational establishments and home economists. Thanks also go to Birds Eye Wall's, Kenwood and Woman's Weekly.

## Picture Credits
With grateful thanks to the Imperial War Museum, and the Radio Times for the illustrations used throughout the book.
Birds Eye Wall's Ltd 31, 77, 89 top.Corbis-Bettmann 69, 94.
Mr P.J. Gouldstone 34.
Reed International Books Ltd. 95.Harpers Bazaar 36.Hulton Getty Picture Collection 5, 7, 12, 15, 20, 29, 42, 70, 79, 85, 88, 101, 107, 109.Kenwood 65.
Robert Opie 6, 17, 27, 46 centre.Marguerite Patten 38 top.Popperfoto 2/3, 11, 22, 32, 48, 51, 52, 58, 61, 72, 78, 82, 92, 97, 98 top, 102.
Sainsbury's Archives 62.